Earth Angel

Memories of Love

By

Andrew Lunn Sr.

ISBN: 1-4140-1512-7 (e-book)
ISBN: 1-4140-1513-5 (Paperback)

This book is printed on acid free paper.

1stBooks - rev. 11/07/03

CONTENTS

FOREWORD

This is a story about two young people who met as teenagers, fell in love and overcame a mountain of adversity to be with one another. Jack and Agnes were destined to be together in what some called a match made in heaven.

This relationship was not without road blocks and setbacks. They survived elements of deception, betrayal and treachery and still managed to salvage their relationship. The pain they suffered left deep scars but the love they shared was enough to sustain them in their quest to be together.

In spite of a difficult start and ongoing tragedies, they remained deeply in love and managed to have a wonderful life together. Their faith in God and love of family and one another was the key that opened the door to their happiness.

AUTHOR'S ACKNOWLEDGMENTS

Thanks to my wife Rita for her patience and support in making this book a success.

Many thanks to Clothilda(Judy)Dingwall for proof reading and editing the book.

CHAPTER ONE

One Special Summer

It was a warm summer day in 1956 in the city of Baltimore, Maryland. Fourteen year old Jack sat quietly on the steps of his west Baltimore row house. It was 8:00 am. and Jack was enjoying one of his quiet moments. This was rare in his house that he shared with his mother and nine siblings. Jack sat quietly flipping through his comic book while he waited for the neighborhood drug store to open. The neighborhood pharmacy was where Jack was employed. He worked there part time during the school year and full time during the summer months. As he turned the pages in his book, he noticed a young person standing in the doorway of a house across the street. This was the first time he noticed her. He was aware that a new family moved into that house. Jack wondered if she were a member of that family.

Suddenly, Jack's sister came to the front door and waved at the girl across the street. She went across the street to engage in a conversation with her. When Jack's sister came back, he asked her who was that young lady? Carolyn responded that her name was

1

Agnes and she moved in the block two weeks ago. She asked Jack if he wanted to meet Agnes and Jack replied, "Not at this time." Jack left for his job at the drug store.

The next morning Jack was standing in his doorway and Agnes appeared at her door. Jack got up enough nerve to wave at her and she smiled and waved back. It was now time for him to go to work. Jack really enjoyed his job at the drug store because it gave him an opportunity to meet and talk with everyone in the neighborhood. He had a very pleasant personality and was very good at helping the customers at the store. He had an outgoing personality that served him well on his job. When it came to meeting girls his own age, Jack was very shy. That was the only time Jack did not have much to say.

Two hours into his shift at the store business was very slow. Jack was day dreaming about the new girl that moved in the neighborhood. He remembered her very pleasant smile and wanted to know more about her. Then, Jack looked up and Agnes was walking into the store. She smiled and asked Jack if he worked here. He informed her that he did and wanted to know if he could be of service. Agnes wanted to know where certain products were. Jack was very knowledgeable about the layout of the store and knew where everything was. He even knew the layout of the pharmacy counter. When Agnes found everything she wanted, Jack dropped what he was doing and waited on her. She smiled at Jack and asked if he were a clerk here? Jack smiled and replied, "I am a clerk, a stock boy, and a cashier all rolled up in one." Jack formally introduced himself and

Agnes did also. Agnes informed Jack that she met his sister (Carolyn) and liked her very much. Agnes completed her purchases and left the store. As she walked across the street, Jack watched her and thought what a wonderful young lady.

A very special feeling came over him. This was unlike any feeling he ever had before. Jack knew many girls from school and from the neighborhood but had never met one that impressed him like Agnes. He could hardly wait to see her smiling face again. When Jack got off from work, he told his sister(Carolyn) that he met the new girl that moved in the block. He asked his sister what she thought about Agnes and what kind of person she was. Carolyn asked why? Do you like her? Without hesitating, Jack replied "No."

He quickly added that he thought she was a very nice young lady and that there was something special about her. Carolyn smiled and asked Jack if he wanted her to put in a good word for him. Jack said to his sister, "No, please don't do that." Carolyn could see that Jack was clearly interested in Agnes.

It was only a couple of weeks before school closed for the summer. Jack would be entering high school in the fall. This was a very special time for Jack because he would be attending a previously segregated high school. That was the prestigious Baltimore City College.

Meantime Jack's sister(Carolyn) and Agnes became very close friends. One day while Carolyn was visiting Agnes, they got into this conversation…you know, girl talk. Agnes began to ask questions about Jack. She told Carolyn that she thought Jack was such a good person. Their conversation continued for a while and Carolyn asked Agnes if she were interested in Jack. Agnes quickly said "No!" It was clear to Carolyn that Agnes was interested in her brother. Carolyn began to tease Agnes and offered to put in a good word for her. Agnes did not want Carolyn to do that, but she later confessed that she liked Jack.

Summer of 1957

When summer arrived, Jack increased his work hours at the neighborhood pharmacy. Jack was an early riser and it was not unusual for him to begin his day at 7:00am. Around 8:00am, he saw Agnes and her sister(Sandy) washing down their marble steps. Jack crossed the street to engage in a conversation with the sisters. Soon, Sandy went inside. Jack and Agnes sat and talked for hours. This became a regular routine for these two young people.

Sometimes, Jack did not leave work until 10:00pm or 11:00pm. He saw Agnes, Sandy and their mother sitting on the steps. First, he stopped by his home, then visited Agnes. Jack spoke to everyone, then took a place on the bottom step next to Agnes. After a short time, Sandy and their mother went inside. Sandy often teased the lovebirds(Jack and Agnes) as she entered the house.

As time progressed, Jack and Agnes grew closer together. Jack could see that Agnes was such a perfect lady with so much character.

For a person her age, she was very mature and knowledgeable. They enjoyed each others company very much. Jack often called her his Earth Angel. He told her he never met a young person as sincere and kind as she was. Agnes was very quiet and reserved with a few close friends. Jack was a hard working, focused young man, who made friends easily.

CHAPTER TWO

...The High School Years...

Summer of 1958

Jack completed his first-year at the prestigious Baltimore City College High School. Jack was a very good student and one of the hand picked students from his all black junior high school to attend City. Jack maintained his honor roll status and was very serious about his education. He liked school and always tried to do his best. Jack wanted to please his mother(Miss Louraine) who stressed education in their family circle. She encouraged her children to strive to be the best they could be. Jack was very close to his mother and became even closer after his parents separated.

Miss Louraine was a very strong black woman who worked very hard to keep her children together. She was strong in her faith and taught her children to trust God and stay focused on their goals. She raised her children practically single handed and worked many jobs to keep her family in tact. Jack's mother was very proud that none of her 10 children had ever given her any serious problems. She taught them to avoid trouble and think about consequences. Jack's mother put the fear of God in them and stated often that he saw everything they did. Jack thought his mother had a direct line to God and could call on him night or day to help keep her children in line.

The attention Jack gave to Agnes did not go unnoticed by his mother. Often, when Agnes visited Jack's sister, his mother had an opportunity to size her up. She was very tactful and shrewd in her line of questioning. Jack was entering his senior year in high school and maintained a B+ average. His mother wanted to make sure he remained focused on his education and not become side tracked. She seemed satisfied that Agnes could be an ally and help to keep Jack on track. She was some what relieved to know that Agnes was a young lady who had character and good morals. She knew her son and how he felt about Agnes. He did not have to say what he was feeling for Agnes but his actions showed that he cared for her very much. His mother wanted to make sure he did not take things too fast.

School year 1959/1960(Graduation)

The school year was the Fall of 1959 and Spring/Summer of 1960. This was the year of Jack's graduation. This was a very important time in Jack's life. His graduating class was one of the largest and the first or second since integration. Most of the black students in Jack's

7

graduating class would make the honor roll. These students were some of the best and brightest from the black community. They paved the way for many others to follow.

Agnes was attending Carver High school where she majored in dress making. She was very proud that Jack was doing well and graduating this year. She understood the importance of his accomplishments. He managed to work at the pharmacy, maintained a B+ average and still share some very precious moments with her. Sometimes it was only a glance in the morning or when she visited the drug store, or a few moments when he left work at night.

Jack's mother noticed the time that Jack was spending with Agnes. Although she had talked with Agnes, and believed she was a decent young lady; she still could see the harm this relationship may have on her son. She knew better than Jack or Agnes the difficulty that young people in love would have in exercising control and good judgement. She thought it was a good time to ask Jack about his plans for the future. Jack's mother asked him about college for the fall of 1960. Jack was very thrifty and knew there would not be any extra money for his college education. He had made plans to attend Morgan State College in September of 1960. He informed his mom that he had already saved his tuition for the first year. She was very relieved to hear that. With a very worried look on her face, she asked him how serious his relationship was with Agnes. Jack was very perceptive and knew exactly where she was going with this line of questioning. He assured her that he was committed to attending and completing college. He also assured her that Agnes was not that kind of young woman and there was no need for her to worry. Jack's mom was pleased with what she heard from her son and decided to drop the topic for now.

Jack grew closer and closer to Agnes. He noticed that she would get sick every month and did not want Jack to see her this way. One day while the two of them were talking and holding hands, Jack asked her why she got sick so much. She told Jack she had female trouble. Jack was very concerned about her and continued to probe for an answer. Agnes decided to explain that each month when her menstrual period came on she got sick. She experienced cramps and became very nauseous. Jack asked if any thing could be done to alleviate the situation. Agnes responded, "I take medication for the sickness and let nature take its course."

Although the explanation was confusing, Jack showed much concern for Agnes. He always planned something very special for her when she felt better. It could be something as simple as taking a walk or going to see a movie. Jack really enjoyed taking Agnes to the movies. He bought a large tub of popcorn and large drinks. He would return to the concession stand and purchase two large candy bars and two hot dogs. The movies were generally good, but even if they were not they always enjoyed the food. It was no secret that the Harlem theater served the best hot dogs in West Baltimore. After finishing their treats, Jack and Agnes cuddled for the remainder of the movie. They enjoyed being close to each other, and Jack held Agnes until his arm got numb. After the movie, they walked home together holding hands. The theater was located only a couple of blocks from where they lived. Everyone in their neighborhood could see that they were an item.

When the couple arrived at Agnes's house, they met Agnes's mother(Miss Helen) and her sister Sandy sitting on the front steps. Jack greeted them and he and Agnes took their position on the lower step. After a while, Miss Helen would get ready to go into the house and called Sandy to come along with her. Sandy would fuss and wanted to know why she had to come in. She said, "After all, I'm older than Agnes." She reluctantly retreated to the doorway and whispered "Good night love birds."

Jack was very fond of Sandy and often teased her. At times, she became angry and chased Jack all over the neighborhood. Agnes watched and smiled, then told Jack not to tease Sandy so much. When Jack and Agnes finally had time alone, they would sit and talk for hours. Other times they would sit and stare at each other.

When Miss Helen came to the second floor window, Agnes knew it was time to come in. Jack would escort Agnes to the doorway to say his good nights. He smiled at her and she took his hand and lead him to the vestibule away from sight. That was the moment Jack was waiting for. They kissed and Agnes asked Jack to hold her. She loved for him to hold her. She felt so secure in his arms.

Jack departed thinking about the kiss he experienced with Agnes. It was like nothing he had ever experienced before. This made him so happy that he literally danced his way across the street to his house.

May 1960

Jack was preparing for his graduation in June. His mother had been giving him driving lessons and he recently received his driver's license. Jack was on the insurance policy with his mother. He was a very responsible young man and was careful not to show off while driving.

Now that Jack had obtained his drivers' license, he was given more responsibility at the pharmacy. Doc trusted him with his car to pick up medications from the wholesale drug company and at times allowed Jack to keep his car over night.

Jack was very mature and responsible when it came to handling his business on his job. Doc noticed these qualities, and asked Jack to collect rents for him when he was too busy to do it. This additional responsibility allowed Jack to explore many parts of the city that he never saw before. Jack possessed good customer relation skills and could collect delinquent rents even when Doc had a problem getting the money. He collected the current rent and accepted partial payments on any delinquent amount. This was something he learned when he used to collect money for the cosmetics his mother sold. Doc was very pleased with the way Jack handled this situation.

It was June of 1960 and Jack's graduation was approaching fast. Jack asked Doc if he could use his car for his senior prom. Doc granted Jack permission without an after thought. He also informed Jack that he could keep the car overnight. Jack and Agnes were looking forward to his senior prom. Agnes made a beautiful gown to wear to the prom. The day before the prom Agnes got very sick. This was the time of the month for her menstrual period. She was devastated when she told Jack she could not attend his senior prom. She was feeling very bad for Jack and could see the hurt and disappointment on his face. Jack wanted to show her off to his school buddies. He talked about her so much to all of his friends.

Although Agnes was very ill, she still was very concerned about Jack making his senior prom. She sprang into action very quickly and asked her best girl friend(Clara) to be Jack's escort for the evening. Clara was a very pretty young woman that lived two doors down from Agnes. She told Agnes that she would be very happy to attend the prom with Jack. Clara's parents and Clara were very fond of Jack and knew he was a responsible and respectable young man. They also knew that Jack was an honor student attending one of the best high schools in the city.

Clara accompanied Jack to his prom and was having a very good time. She met many of Jack's friends. They told Jack what a pretty young woman she was. Jack quickly informed them that his girl friend took ill and Clara was a very good friend of hers who was standing in for her. One of Jack's Jewish friends invited them to a

12

party in Pikesville after the prom. Jack was very pleased but declined the invitation. Clara was impressed with Jack's friends and really wanted to attend the party. Jack told Clara that he promised her parents he would bring her home right after the prom. Jack convinced Clara that he made the right decision. Jack was really thinking about Agnes and how she was feeling.

Clara and Jack arrived in the block after the prom. Jack noticed Agnes up in the second floor window of her house. Clara did not see her. Jack escorted Clara to her house and thanked her parents for letting her attend his prom. Right away, Clara began to tell her parents about all the wonderful friends Jack had. She told them that they were invited to a party in Pikesville. Clara's father interrupted her saying "Pikesville, no colored people live out there." Clara said it was one of Jack's Jewish friends. Clara advised her parents that Jack declined because he wanted to get her back at a decent hour. Clara's mother chimed in that Jack is such a gentleman. It would have been all right if you had called to let us know. Jack could not wait to leave, he promised to show them all the pictures when they were developed. He said his good byes and left.

He went straight to Agnes's house and looked up at the second floor window. She was still looking out the window. Jack signaled for her to come down. In a few minutes, her door opened and she asked him to come in. It was a little after midnight, and everyone else in the house was asleep. They sat in her living room and talked quietly. Jack asked her how she felt. I'm still feeling quite sick but

I'm better now that I see you. Agnes wanted to know all about the prom and if they had a good time. Jack responded, "Clara really had a good time but all I could do was to think about you." They embraced and Jack held her in his arms for quite a while. Jack heard Agnes's mother moving about upstairs, then she called out to see where Agnes was. Agnes replied, "I am in the living room talking to Jack." Miss Helen yelled down to Jack greeting him and asked how was the prom. Jack said it was okay. She did not say anything else. She was a lady of few words. Jack could sense that it was all right to sit and talk a bit longer.

Jack told Agnes how proud he was of her. He thought what a courageous thing she did by asking Clara to attend his prom so his evening would not be spoiled. Even in her sickness, she was still very much concerned about Jack not being totally disappointed on his prom night. Jack told her what a special person she was. He held her for a little while longer and then kissed her good night.

CHAPTER THREE

Jack enters college

September 1960 — Jack enters college

Jack was now a freshman at Morgan State College. Jack continued his employment at the pharmacy while taking a full load at school. College life was a lot different from high school. Jack soon found out that the courses were more demanding and required a great deal of time and focus.

Jack met a lot of interesting students from all over the United States and some foreign countries. He made new friends, many from other east coast cities and other counties in Maryland. There were many counties in Maryland that Jack never visited or met anyone from. He met a young man from Sykesville(a small town in Carroll County, Md) named James. James quickly became one of Jack's closest friends.

James lived with his grandmother in Sykesville. Once he started school at Morgan, He moved in with his mother in Baltimore City. This was around the corner from Jack's house. James needed a part time job for additional income. With a recommendation from Jack, James was able to get a job at the pharmacy. This made the bond between Jack and James even closer.

Jack did not see Agnes as much as he wanted to because of the full schedule at school and the hours he worked. Agnes was preparing to graduate from high school. Jack asked her about plans to continue her education. He wanted to know if she was interested in college. Agnes responded that she had no immediate plans to attend college. She expressed concerns that she needed to find a full time job to help out with family expenses. Her father lost his job and the family was going through some difficult times.

Agnes confided in Jack, explaining that her father was not able to keep a job very long because of his drinking problem. Her mother was ill and not able to work. Her sister Sandy dropped out of high school when she became pregnant. She lost the baby, but was not prepared to go to work at that time. Agnes was very mature and practical and knew that she had to accept the responsibility of helping her family meet their obligations. Jack understood and did not pressure Agnes with any more questions on her education.

Agnes and Jack were going steady for three years and did not have any sex during that time. They came very close a few times, but Agnes always managed to keep her head about such matters and remind Jack that he needed to stay focused on completing his education. She reminded Jack that she would always be there for him and the sex could wait for now. She was always being teased by her sister(Sandy) about being a virgin and being called "Miss goody two shoes." Agnes would smile and ignore her sister.

Agnes was very proud of Jack attending Morgan, and seemed especially pleased to see him dressed in his Army R.O.T.C. uniform.

She watched as Jack and James walked down the street in their uniforms carrying stacks of books. James often told Jack how lucky he was to have such a caring and mature young lady. Jack smiled and say "yeah".

Jack cared for Agnes very much and tried not to pressure her into having sex. He found it very difficult to be around her and touch her and to suppress his natural feelings toward her. Agnes was constantly thinking about Jack's future and tried very hard to assure him that she too found it very difficult to be with him and not think of engaging in sex. She also knew how Jack's mother felt about him. They both wanted Jack to complete his education without any distractions. Jack had an older brother and two older sisters that attended college before him but did not complete their education without interruptions. Jack's mother wanted to make sure Jack would be the first to go through school uninterrupted.

Jack's mother knew he cared a lot for Agnes. She liked the way Agnes carried herself and considered her a gracious young lady. When Agnes visited Jack's house to see his sister his mother had an opportunity to talk to her. Jack always came up in the conversation. Jack's mother was very persistent and very protective of not only Jack but all of her children. Agnes was very perceptive and knew where this line of questioning was going. She assured Jack's mom that they were not engaging in sex and that she wanted the same thing for Jack that she wanted. Agnes informed Jack's mother that she would remain in control and was very much concerned about his future.

Jack stopped putting pressure on Agnes to have sex but that did not stop him from wanting it. He continued to work at the drug store which gave him an opportunity to meet a lot of people from the neighborhood. They all respected him and admired his friendliness and positive attitude. They saw him as a young man that was going places. Many in the area saw him as a good catch for their daughter, niece, sister or even for themselves.

The Web

Across the street from the drug store, lived a couple that visited the store often. They were very friendly to Jack and at times would be a few cents short on their purchase. Jack often loaned them the difference from his pocket. They always paid him back on the return visit. One day a customer entered the store with a younger girl in her teens. She seemed to be around Agnes's age. She was very pretty and very well built. The older lady (Liz) introduced the young girl as her baby sister. Her name was Cora. She noticed Jack looking at her

18

and gave him a big smile. Jack turned his head away because he did not want it to appear that he was staring at her. Liz informed Jack that Cora came to live with her and her husband since their mother had recently died.

Cora began coming to the drug store on a regular basis and engaged Jack in conversation. Agnes was now working at a clothing factory and her family had moved about a half mile away from the drug store. Jack was still very much in love with Agnes but because of their busy schedules, he did not see her very often. When he did see her it was generally on the week end. She always seemed to be very tired and was still getting sick a lot. They both cherished the precious moments they shared when they were together. They spent most of their time sitting and talking to each other with Jack holding her. Agnes was practically taking care of her family with some help from her older brothers. They gave her mother money to help with expenses. Her father was not working at all at this time and his drinking had gotten worse.

Agnes loved her father very much and explained that he was very good to her when she was a little girl. She was the only one who could get him to do anything. He was a very intelligent man that always seemed to wind up with menial jobs that he despised. Jack was very impressed with her father's intelligence. They got along rather well. This pleased Miss Helen as well as Agnes.

Mean time, Cora was making daily visits to the drug store that was a pharmacy, liquor outlet and convenience store all wrapped into one. Sometimes, she was very scantily dressed and knew Jack was watching her. She was very well built and liked to tease Jack. Jack could see everything going on in the neighborhood from his vantage point in the drug store. The store had very large windows and was conveniently located on the corner over looking the entire neighborhood.

Every evening at sunset the neighbors came out and sat on their front steps. This was a favorite summer pass time. Everyone was clean and neatly dressed. Jack noticed Cora sitting on her steps in very tight short pants. He noticed an older man came by on a regular basis and picked her up. He drove up to her house in his powder blue Cadillac, blew his horn and she got into the car and they drove off.

The next time Cora came into the store she was not as jolly as she had been. Jack could see that something was bothering her. Jack was a good listener and was always willing to help anyone. Cora asked Jack what time he got off from work and could he stop by her house on his way home. His friend(James) over heard the conversation and told Jack to be careful where that girl was concerned. It was quite obvious that James did not care for Cora very much.

Jack told James, "Thanks man, I'm cool."

Jack left work that night and Cora was sitting on her front steps. She was dressed in very tight short pants exposing her very shapely legs. She also had on a tight tee shirt showing off her grapefruit size well developed breasts. Jack had one thing on his mind but did not want to move too fast and over play his hand. Cora began the conversation while Jack listened to what seemed like a troubled young lady. After a while, Cora seemed more relaxed. Jack continued to listen as she opened up more and more.

Finally, Cora told Jack what was bothering her. She told Jack that she was pregnant by a married man and did not know what to do. She had just met Jack, but felt she could trust him with such a personal secret. She had not shared this information with her sister. Jack asked her if the guy knew about her situation. Cora stated that he knew and was not very happy about it. He was the man that used to pick her up in the blue cadillac. This fellow (T.J.) told her he would pay for an abortion for her. Cora was very worldly, and happy go lucky but this obviously bothered her very much. Jack told her that this was a decision that she had to make for herself. Whatever she decided to do, she had to live with that decision for the rest of her life.

Jack did not see Cora again until two weeks later. She told Jack thanks for being a friend. She also informed him that she decided to get the abortion after discussing the situation with her sister. Cora decided not to see the married man again. Then, out of the blue she asked Jack if he had a girl friend. Jack responded "Yes I do have a girl friend." Just as quickly as she asked, she dropped the matter.

Cora noticed that Jack had been looking at her body whenever he thought she was not aware. She began to tease Jack and asked him if he thought she was pretty. I think you are a very attractive young lady. During the conversation, Jack picked up on the fact that Cora was very experienced for a girl her age. Cora then stood directly in front of Jack profiling her body. She strutted up and down the street swerving her body teasing Jack. Jack smiled and tried to play it off.

Summer 1961

A few days went by and Jack was at work in the drug store. The sun was beginning to set. The residents of the neighborhood started to take up their positions on their steps. Cora was sitting on her front steps. It was between 7:30 and 8:00 pm when Jack noticed Agnes coming up the street towards the drug store. Agnes entered the store and began a conversation with Jack. Jack was very pleased that Agnes stopped by because they were not seeing a lot of each other. Her job at the sewing factory required her to get up at six in the morning. It was a very hard job and quite demanding. Jack walked Agnes to the sidewalk outside the drug store. Agnes asked Jack to come to see her on the week end. During the week she went to bed very early. She kissed Jack on the cheek and walked up the street. Jack watched her all the way up the street.

Mean while, Cora was still sitting on her steps taking it all in. It was close to 10:30pm when Jack left the drug store. Cora called him as he was crossing the street. She asked Jack if that was his girl friend he was talking to. Jack stated that it was. Cora asked Jack to sit and talk to her for awhile. She asked Jack if he had ever been to a night club. Jack said he had not. She informed Jack that she had been to a place outside of the city that served food and drinks and had an outside dance floor. She asked Jack if he could go for a ride. Jack said sure he could.

Jack had his license and was on his mother's insurance. He did not want it to appear that he had to get permission to go out or drive his mother's car. He told Cora to wait on her steps while he go home to change his shirt. Jack knew that his mother would be asleep or getting ready to go to bed. He went into the house, changed his shirt and made sure everything was quiet.

He picked up the car and drove to get Cora. She had gone into her house to change clothes and came out looking really beautiful. Jack asked her where she wanted to go. Cora asked if he knew how to get to Ritchie Hwy. Jack said he sure did. When they got to Ritchie Hwy, Cora told him to continue down the road for a mile or so and make a left at Cedar Hill Lane. Cedar Hill Lane was a narrow road with woods on both sides. It was very dark until they reached an area where there was a car park. Then, they saw the dance floor on the outside with lights all around it. Jack was not aware this was where he was taking Cora. He had never seen anything like it.

There was a building that the night club was located in. You could order your drinks here and also pick up food orders. The dance floor looked like a large boxing ring that was roped off. Cora looked at Jack and said welcome to the Forest. This was the name of the club. The music was blasting and couples were all over the dance floor.

Jack did not go to a lot of dances, but knew all of the latest steps by practicing with his sisters. He was really a very good dancer. This type of club was a new experience for Jack but Cora seemed to know her way around very well. The music was loud but very good to dance to. Cora grabbed Jack by the hand and led him to the dance floor. Jack loosened up and they really swung to the live music of the band. Jack was having a good time, but noticed it was after midnight. Jack knew he would have to leave soon. He asked Cora if she was hungry. Cora stated that she could eat a little something. By this time, it was 1:00am. Jack bought some sodas and barbecue ribs and they left.

As they drove back to town, Cora told Jack that she was very impressed with his dancing. She said," Not bad for a bookworm". She informed Jack that she had a very good time with him. She asked Jack to come in and eat some ribs. Jack said he would park his mother's car and would be right back. Jack parked the car and ran into his house to make sure everything was all right. The house was quiet and everyone was still asleep. Jack did not like the idea of sneaking around, but he seemed somewhat mystified by this glamorous young woman. Jack quietly closed the door and headed back to Cora's house.

Jack walked the half block to Cora's house and let himself in. Cora shared the apartment with her sister's family. She had a bedroom in the rear of the apartment which had a separate entrance. Cora and Jack began eating the ribs when she remembered she had a couple of beers in the fridge. She asked Jack if he would like one. "Don't mind if I do," replied Jack. Jack was not a big drinker but occasionally he would indulge himself. They ate the ribs and drank a couple of beers. Jack was aware that it was approaching 2:00am and was not used to being out this late. Again, Cora thanked Jack for a very good evening. She could tell that Jack was getting a little nervous and decided to play with him a little.

They stood up to finish their good night greetings when Cora moved her body very close to Jack. She put her arms around Jack's neck and told him once again, "Thanks for a wonderful time." Cora took Jack by the hand and told him she wanted to show him a picture in her room. When they entered the room, Cora turned abruptly and kissed him. She caught Jack completely off guard. She smiled and kissed him again, this time Jack kissed her back. Jack was a very good kisser, in fact that was about the extent of his experience.

Cora pulled Jack's body even closer. What started out as a tease began to get serious. She enjoyed the feeling of his young strong body next to hers. Jack felt his heart racing and his private part began to throb. He caressed her soft shapely body and began kissing all over her face and neck. Cora felt the hardness of his body and how it was throbbing. She looked Jack straight in the eye and said, "Poor baby." She took off her blouse and Jack could not move. Next, she peeled off her bra exposing her very shapely grape fruit sized breasts. Jack began to perspire. Cora told him to take off his clothes and get comfortable. She could see that he did not have much experience in these matters and began to help him get undressed. Cora then finished getting undressed and the two began to hold each other very close. They kissed and she pulled him on the bed. Jack caressed her lips and kissed her breasts as his hands wandered all over her luscious body sparing not even her most private parts. Jack laid upon her body as she guided his magnificent organ into her inner parts. She told Jack not to be nervous and to take his time. She controlled her movements and guided him to the parts of her body satisfying both of their cravings. Tonight she was his teacher and he was a willing and able student. With his organ as hard as steel, his deep thrusts into her soft warm caverns produced sensations that he had never before experienced. Cora began to moan and groan asking for more, more. Jack did his best to answer her beckoning call going deep into her body trying to touch her soul. The warm heat of her body and the gyrating motions began to draw the sap from his body with a jerking motion. The sweet nectar was flowing like water, when she cried out, "Oh sweet daddy, Oh sweet daddy." Jack knew at that moment he was getting the job done. They rested in each others arms for a while; then, Jack got dressed to leave. Cora just laid there in the bed. It was now 3:30am. Jack left and quietly entered his house being careful not to wake anyone.

Jack slept the next day until 12:00 noon. His brother woke him up and asked him what time he was going to work today. Jack said he was working from 2:00 to 10:00pm. He could not believe it was already 12:00 noon. Jack got up and took a bath thinking about what he experienced the night before. This pleasurable feeling soon led way to guilt. Jack really wanted to have this experience with Agnes. He knew she was saving herself for him and trying to wait until they were both ready to make a total commitment. Initially, Jack thought by having sex with Cora he did not have to pressure Agnes. He felt very satisfied but at the same time he knew he betrayed the trust Agnes had in him.

Cora knew how Jack felt about Agnes and she also knew according to Jack that Agnes was not putting out. She could see that Jack was a decent young man but had needs that she was willing and able to fulfill. After four hours into his shift at work, Jack saw Cora come to her front steps in a very sexy outfit. He could see guys in the neighborhood approaching her but it appeared that she would not give them the time of day. Cora's sister came into the drug store to buy some beer and kept smiling at Jack. Jack spoke to her and smiled back. She then told Jack that I heard that you and Cora had a good time last night. Jack just smiled and said yeah. He was now wondering how many other people knew about last night. When she left the store, James approached Jack and said what was all that about? James looked at Jack and said," No you didn't. Did you, ah hell man?" What's wrong with you? Jack just turned and walked away.

Jack walked back to James and said, "Hey man I do have some needs." James responded, "I just don't feel she is right for you." I think she is too wild. Jack stated," For the time being she is supplying my needs, nothing serious."

CHAPTER FOUR

Trapped

Cora now felt like Jack was a fish on a hook that could be pulled in any time she wanted him. She knew how much he desired her and used this to manipulate him. Cora thought she was in complete control as long as she kept the relationship hot and interesting. She introduced Jack to the night life and the party scene. Jack enjoyed the excitement of being with Cora, but never felt this relationship was going to get serious. Cora mentioned to Jack that she did not want a serious relationship either. Although Jack was living a lie, he thought he was in a win win situation. He was unaware of the trouble he was headed for.

This went on for months and Jack was seeing less and less of Agnes. People in the neighborhood began to talk. They knew in spite of Jack's reckless behavior, he was a decent young man. Many thought he was being manipulated by a very promiscous and worldly young woman. Eventually, word of his escapades got back to his mother. One evening before Jack left work, Cora stopped by the drug store and told him that she wanted to see him. She told Jack to bring some scotch with him when he came over.

Jack stopped by to talk with Cora a little while. He was not very talkative or his usual out going self. Cora asked him what was wrong. Jack informed her that he would not be able to see her as much. Cora interrupted him asking if his perfect little earth angel was giving him pressure. Jack said, "No, worst than that. My mother is on to our relationship." "So what, "Cora snapped. I guess she doesn't like me. She asked Jack to pour her a drink of scotch. Jack did so and also poured one for himself. Normally, Jack would not drink any hard liquor unless it was a very special occasion. After taking a drink or two, Cora decided to see if she could still work her magic on Jack. She asked Jack if she meant anything at all to him? Jack responded, "Of course you do," but we will need to be more discreet. You mean you want me to be your night time play thing. Jack did not respond but just stared at her. Cora then smiled at Jack and asked him to come closer. She asked Jack if he would hold her for a moment. Cora started to kiss Jack and he responded very passionately. The next thing Jack knew he was like a fly trapped in a spider's web.

Cora began to undress and expose her beautiful body. Jack found her irresistible. Before he could think straight, he was taking off his clothes. She beconked for him to come closer. He was like a slave obeying his master. Once again, he found himself having wild passionate sex with her. This was one very strong hold that she had on Jack and had no problem using it. After making love, Cora told

Jack she really liked the way he made her feel. She never had anyone as decent as Jack. What started out as a game to her evolved into a very special relationship.

This kind of talk confused Jack. He enjoyed being with Cora and was not interested in converting her or changing her attitude towards life. When Jack met her, she was very hard hearted because of certain conditions that existed in her life. She was a survivor with a devil may care attitude. Initially, she was not interested in any commitments. She never experienced anyone as kind or caring as Jack. On the other hand, Jack never experienced anyone like Cora. Until this relationship, Jack led a very sheltered life. Cora really turned Jack out. Cora used her sex appeal like a weapon. She knew she was beautiful and felt that her beauty and sex appeal was all she needed to get what she wanted. This attitude began to change when Jack came on the scene. She discovered that Jack was caring, loving and basically a very good person. She felt that this relationship was not going to last. She had fallen in love with Jack and tried very hard to mask her true feelings with her nonchalant attitude.

Jack was interested in Cora because she brought excitement to his life. He still cared and loved Agnes very much, but knew she did not approve of premarital sex. Agnes was also the type of girl that Jack could present to his mother or any other significant person in his life. What Jack did not count on was how much he was addicted to the good sex Cora was providing to him.

Jack and Cora sat up all night talking and listening to each other. Jack consumed more alcohol than the normal beer or two. Before long they fell asleep. When they woke up, it was well past 8:00am. Jack was ready to rush home, but Cora convinced him to stay for breakfast. After breakfast, Jack said he would do the dishes.

While Jack was doing the dishes, there was a very loud knock on Cora's door. She opened the door to see who was there. Suddenly, there was this loud commotion and this voice that asked, Is my son in here? Cora did not know what to say. Jack's mother(Miss Louraine) pushed her way into the apartment and entered the kitchen. She really tore into Jack. Look at you, you big fool. Why are you in here with this tramp? Leave this place right now! Jack was so embarrassed. He told his mother that he would be home in a moment. His mother looked at him in total disgust. Jack felt like finding a hole and crawling into it. He turned to Cora and asked, why did you let her in. Cora replied," When I opened the door, she pushed right pass me yelling Is my son in here?" I was so frightened I did not know what to do. I never saw a look like that on anyone's face before.

I know what you mean. My mother can be ferocious when it comes to the welfare of her children. He knew that Cora was no match for his mom. Cora replied "After all, it was your mother," What else could I do?. Then she said to Jack sarcasticly, you are twenty years old aren't you? Jack knew he had to face the music when he got home. Unlike Cora, there were consequences for Jack's action.

When Jack got home the house was buzzing. Jack heard his mother and four of his siblings discussing the incident. Jack's mother wanted him to be embarrassed and feel shame. She certainly accomplished this. When there was a problem with any of her children, she would hold court with all of them. She felt they all had the responsibility to look out for each other and to let her know when one was going astray. She told the others how foolish Jack looked standing there in Cora's kitchen doing her dirty dishes.

Jack's mother stated again that Cora was a tramp, and no decent girl would keep a young man out all night. She asked," Jack, what were you thinking?" Jack did not say one word in his defense. Then she told Jack that he ought to be ashamed because he was seeing a very respectable girl like Agnes. Miss Louraine knew that Agnes was not the type of girl to have sex and keep him out all night. Again, she asked Jack what happened? He tried to tell her without all of the sorted details. He told his mother that he and Cora were sitting up playing cards and fell asleep. He also told her that she was not a tramp. In spite of all that happened, Jack cared for Cora and had fun with her. She was filling a crucial need that Jack enjoyed very much.

Guilt and Betrayal

Jack felt quite guilty that he betrayed Agnes. He respected her wishes to not pressure her for sex. There were times when they both wanted to break that promise and had come pretty close to it. Agnes

33

was the stronger of the two and a very wise and practical young lady. She wanted to keep Jack's mother as an ally. She was no fool, she knew that if she destroyed that trust she would have hell to pay. She also knew how Jack felt about his mother and did not want to be responsible for damaging that relationship. This arrangement worked well for Agnes because she was a deeply religious young lady and did not believe in sex before marriage. She truly loved Jack and had his best interest at heart. She had to be stronger than Jack for both of their sake.

Jack knew that he had to repair the damage done to the relationship he had with his mother. They shared a very special bond. A bond that became even closer when Jack's father left the family. This was the single most important person in his life. He did not keep many things from his mother but he certainly could not share his escapades with Cora with her. His mother was extremely hurt and disappointed in him and did not try to hide that fact. Jack knew that nothing was worth him risking the love he felt for his mother and the love she felt for him. He knew he had to end his relationship with Cora. Cora was younger than Jack, but taught him many things about life. Most of them were bad.

Jack put some distance between himself and Cora and was very careful not to go to her apartment again. Jack noticed that Agnes began to visit his home more. She said she came to visit Jack's sister who was her close friend. Jack's mother seemed pleased with this arrangement. Jack was still feeling guilty and wondered if Agnes knew anything about his relationship with Cora. Although Jack saw Cora mostly at night, she never tried to hide her feelings for Jack when she visited him during the day at the drug store. She did not care who knew how she felt about Jack, and certainly did not hide her feelings.

When Jack stopped his visits to Cora, she visited him at the drug store. While he was talking to Cora, he noticed Agnes approaching the store. He asked his friend (James) to talk to Cora for awhile. James could see what was about to happen and took Cora by the hand and led her to the rear of the store. Agnes came into the store with her pleasant attitude and refreshing smile. Jack smiled and began to talk to her. Agnes informed Jack that she was off from work a couple of days because things were slow at the factory. She asked Jack if he wanted to do anything special and to stop pass her house when he gets off from work. Jack agreed, but had a sinking feeling that Agnes knew more than she was letting on.

Meanwhile, Cora was in the rear of the store looking at greeting cards. When Agnes left, Cora approached Jack with a devilish smirk on her face. How is mama's boy now that he has had a visit from his angel? Jack looked at Cora, but did not dignify that remark with an answer. Then, Cora blurted out," How do you think that makes me feel?" You only want to see me at night because miss angel pooh ain't giving it up. Besides, I have something very important to discuss with you. You really need to stop by and talk with me. Suddenly, all of the smart talk was gone and a look of desperation came over her face. Jack knew something was brewing. He felt as if he was sitting on a powder keg ready to blow. When the pharmacy closed later that night, James asked Jack if he wanted to stop by his place and listen to his new albums by Miles Davis and the M.J.Q. (Modern Jazz Quartet). Jack replied, "Not tonight buddy, I have a full course on my plate." James told Jack to be careful and get it together. I care about you. I know, Jack replied.

Jack quickly crossed the street and stopped by Cora's place. I can't stay long, but I want to know what's on your mind. What's the matter, do you have a date? Don't be cruel, Jack replied. "Well", Cora said, "Since you are in a hurry I'll get right to the point." You have not been around to see me and I need to discuss something with you. This is the second month that I have missed my menstrual period. Do you know what that means? Jack knew exactly what it meant but did not answer. "Cat got your tongue," Cora quipped. Then she just blurted it out, "I am pregnant Jack." Jack asked are you sure? Cora told Jack, "I am pregnant with your child, what are you going to do." What do you want me to do, Cora? What do people generally do in a case like this. Jack asked Cora what are you trying to say? I want us to be a family, Jack. "Wait a minute," Jack answered, "Stop right there." I am not ready for no family. Cora confronted Jack, you don't think I'm good enough for you. I know your mother don't care for me but I think I can make you happy. Jack could see that Cora was upset and he certainly did not want to hurt her even more. He told her he needed some time to think on this matter. She told him not to take too long because she needed an answer soon.

Jack left and went straight home. He had just been hit with a bomb shell. He knew he would not be good company for Agnes tonight. He phoned her to let her know he was not feeling well and would not be stopping by. She told Jack to take care of himself and get some rest. Jack felt bad telling Agnes a lie. She was such a decent and sweet person. He had never met anyone as honest and caring as she was. He wondered how he got himself in such a mess. Agnes was always very considerate of others. Jack often told her that she was too good for this earth.

Jack stayed in his room that night playing Jazz albums. He often did this when he wanted to relax or think about something. He did not know how to tell Cora that he was not ready to be a father. Jack did not want to tell her he was not in love with her. He decided to write Cora a letter. Jack was looking for a pen that worked and at that moment could only find one that wrote in red ink. He chose his words very carefully, because he did not want to make a bad situation worst. Jack expressed how good Cora made him feel when they went out together. She was very sassy, sexy and full of life. She certainly fulfilled some of his needs as well as her own. Jack expressed concerns about the responsibility of fatherhood. He also pointed out that he did not believe either of them would make good parents at this juncture in their lives. He suggested in the letter that she might want to consider doing what she did when he first met her. He would get whatever amount of money she needed to have it done. Jack informed Cora that he was writing this letter because it was too painful to tell her these things in person. He emphasized that he cared for her, but not like what she envisioned. He stated he was willing to help her with whatever decision she made, but he wanted to continue his education. Jack stopped short of telling her he was not in love with her. He knew she was not the kind of girl he wanted to marry, but he could not tell her that she was merely fulfilling his sexual needs. She gave the impression that she was satisfied with the relationship they had without any commitments. Little did he know she had fallen in love with him. He showed her some good times as well as her showing him some very exciting moments. This was a good lesson and learning experience for Jack, and he knew now that he could not treat sex so casually.

Three or four weeks went by and Jack did not see or hear anything from Cora. One day she stopped in the drug store and asked Jack if he would stop by to see her. Jack was ambivalent but knew this was something he needed to do. Later that evening, Jack paid Cora a visit. Cora told him that the situation was taken care of. She explained to Jack that under the circumstances, she decided to have the abortion. Jack was obviously pleased, but felt very bad for Cora. He offered to pay the entire cost, but Cora only accepted half. She told him, after all she was half the blame. Cora was not her usual bubbly self. She was subdued and looked very sad. Jack consoled her. He told her how bad he felt for her and was willing to help her anyway he could to get through this crisis. She informed Jack that he was the only thing she wanted or needed. Then, she said, "Too bad you don't feel the same way about me." Suddenly, she broke out in laughter and said, "I was only kidding myself to think that I could hold on to this college boy." Jack said his goodbyes and left.

CHAPTER FIVE

...A New Beginning...

Summer Of 1962

Jack completed his second full year of college. He matured very quickly over the last couple of months He decided to take a couple of courses during the summer to remain focused on his education. Jack did not see Agnes very often, but when he did it was very special. It was very difficult on Jack now that he had developed a sexual appetite. He tried hard not to put any pressure on Agnes to have sex, but found it extremely difficult. It was also very hard on Agnes.

There were times when she wanted very much to have sex with Jack, but felt the time was not right. Agnes always managed to control the situation and not let it go too far. Jack respected Agnes for her strong values and chose not to put undue pressure on her.

One day, Agnes finally told Jack she knew he had sex with that wild girl but did not choose to confront him with the issue. Jack remained very quiet and did not say a word. She told Jack she wanted him so bad, but thought of the consequences of the act. She prayed that she would not lose him and that he would come to his senses. Jack looked at her amazed and thought to himself that she is just too good for this world. She is truly an angel.

Because of their busy schedules, Jack and Agnes did not see each other very often. By September of 1962, Jack had entered his third year of college. He focused more on his studies. He grew farther and farther away from Agnes. Not because he did not care for her, but because he cared so much. It was so difficult for Jack to be around Agnes and not touch her. When Jack did see her they would cuddle and hug for hours. Eventually, this would lead to Jack trying to take things to far. He did not want to hurt Agnes by constantly putting her in an awkward situation, but he simply could not help himself. For a while, Jack just stopped seeing Agnes altogether.

Weeks went by and the weeks turned into months. Jack was not seeing anyone else, but was simply burying himself in his studies. It was not easy for Jack to stay focused on his schoolwork. Even though he was not seeing Agnes, she was constantly on his mind. Agnes had not seen or heard from Jack for awhile. She did not know what to think. Meanwhile, a high school classmate of Agnes stopped by to chat with her. He was a quiet young man that used to walk her home from school. He soon enlisted in the Army and asked Agnes to write to him. On his leave from the military, Sammy stopped by to see Agnes. Sammy wanted more than a platonic relationship with

Agnes. He wanted to know if she was still involved with Jack. Sammy informed Agnes that she is the type of lady he would like to marry. Sammy asked Agnes to consider this a proposal. He did not expect an answer right away, but asked her to think about it.

Agnes stopped by the drug store to see Jack. She told Jack that she had been communicating by letters to this guy named Sammy. She told Jack that Sammy was on leave and wanted to visit her. She did not see the harm in him visiting. She just saw him as a friend. Agnes always saw the good in people. She trusted people and was very honest. Jack asked Agnes why she was telling him all of this? Agnes stated that Sammy wanted to know if she was involved with anyone. She told him that she was. Agnes then told Jack that this guy asked her to marry him. Jack could not believe what he was hearing. He was speechless. Agnes told Jack that she was not interested in Sammy but befriended him. She had not seen Jack for months and wanted to know where they stood. Jack did not say very much, but clearly he was devastated. He decided to stop by and see Agnes later that evening. Jack knocked on Agnes's door and Sammy opened the door. Who would you like to see? Certainly not you, Where is Agnes? Sammy gave Jack a very mean look. Jack looked at Sammy and asked him" Are you thinking about getting that uniform dirty"? At that moment, Agnes appeared as Jack was about to leave. Please don't leave Jack. I was just explaining to Sammy that I could not marry him because I am in love with you. She was so glad to see Jack, and told him that she would handle this situation. She asked

42

Jack to trust her. Jack decided to let Agnes handle the situation. He informed her that he would return later. Jack realized at that moment how much he really loved Agnes. He blamed himself for not paying the attention to Agnes that was necessary to prevent the very situation she found herself in. Jack walked and walked for what seemed like an eternity thinking of how he almost let the girl he truly love slip through his fingers.

A couple of hours went by and Jack returned to Agnes's house. When Jack entered, Agnes asked Jack to hold her and never let her go. She told Jack she missed him so much and was afraid she had lost him. Jack told Agnes that she was always on his mind but failed to communicate his feelings to her. He also confessed to her how difficult it was being close to her and not making advances toward her. He thought somehow by staying away from her he was not putting pressure on her. Agnes burst out in tears and told Jack, she thought he did not love her anymore. That's when she began to answer the letters that Sammy was sending her. She was sorry that she did not approach Jack sooner. Jack embraced her and they kissed for the longest time.

Agnes decided at that moment that she would not let Jack get away from her again. She informed Jack that she would do whatever it takes to prove her love for him including having sex. Jack knew that she was speaking from her heart. He finally heard what he always thought he wanted to hear. But somehow it did not seem right. He told Agnes that he wanted her more than anything else on this earth but he did not want to pressure her this way. He wanted it to come naturally and without any pressure. He knew he truly loved her, not just for her body but for the decent and loving human being that she was. Jack was aware that there was a difference in just having sex and having sex with someone you truly love. For the remainder of the evening, Jack and Agnes held each other very close and could hear their hearts beating above their quiet conversation. They fell asleep in each other's arms.

Starting Over

The relationship that Jack and Agnes shared grew stronger and stronger. They spent all of their spare time together. They were as committed as a couple could be without being married. After missing Jack's high school prom and his first R.O.T.C. ball, Agnes got a chance to show off her dressmaking skills at the big R.O.T.C. Ball. She made a stunning gown and had all the charm to really set it off. Jack's friends were really impressed with her charm and beauty. Jack was so proud of Agnes as he showed her off to all of his college buddies. They were happy to be in love and together. This was one of their shinning moments.

Jack enjoyed going to jazz concerts and would take her every chance he got. The time Jack was spending with Agnes did not escape his mother's watchful eye. But after Jack's fiasco with Cora, his mom remained low keyed for the time being. Agnes mother's family was having a family reunion in Bowie, Md. Most of her family members would be attending but Agnes declined the invitation this year. She had some dressmaking projects that she decided to spend her time on. Her parents and her sister were driven to the reunion by an older brother. Agnes worked on her project for a little while and called Jack. She asked Jack if he wanted to spend some time with her. Jack picked up a pizza, snacks and soft drinks. When he arrived, he asked where everyone was. Agnes replied they were at the family reunion in Bowie.

Jack and Agnes ate the pizza and snacks and relaxed in the living room. They played music and talked for awhile. Agnes asked Jack if he would just hold her? She wanted him to be close to her. Jack asked if everything was alright. Agnes needed to be assured of his love for her. She felt good whenever he was near her. Once again, Jack confessed his love for her. He told her he never wanted anything to come between them again. They sat there on the couch reassuring each other of their love. They kissed and looked into each others eyes and embraced.

They continued to kiss and talk to each other. Jack started to rub and touch Agnes and became aroused. He caressed her breast and felt her soft warm body in the most private places.

Only, this time he noticed that she did not resist or try to restrain him. She told him she wanted him to make love to her. They continued to kiss and touch each other for a few more moments. Agnes took Jack by the hand and led him up to her bedroom. She looked at Jack and told him that she was trying to wait for them to get married first, but she felt now was the right time. Jack did not say very much because he wanted Agnes so much. Jack was very gentle and took his time with Agnes because he wanted this to be a very special and enjoyable experience for her. They were not disappointed. They made love and this was indeed a very wonderful experience for two people who were truly in love. After they made love they returned to the living room to talk and hold each other.

Agnes knew she had crossed over into territory where she had not been before and was totally committed to Jack. Jack confessed his love for her and pledged to always stick by her. He knew this was the woman he planned to marry and have a family with. Jack also knew that he had to stay focused on completing his education. They both agreed to be sensible about their relationship and be very discreet. Anyone that knew them or saw them together could easily tell that these were two people that were very much in love. They went every place together and did everything together.

Agnes always found a way to visit Jack's home. She went there to visit his sister but would always remain until Jack came home. When Jack arrived, they slipped out and Jack walked Agnes home and spent some time with her. Agnes shared an experience with Jack on a recent visit with his sister. Jack's mother entered into a conversation with her. She really wanted to know if the relationship between her and Jack remained the same. By that she meant, was their relationship still free from sex. Agnes did not want to lie to

Jack's mom so she just implied that things were the same. Jack understood and certainly did not want his mother to know that he was having sex with Agnes. He and Agnes agreed that they would have to be very careful.

The time that Jack and Agnes spent together was really quality time. They both had a very busy schedule. Jack with his school and job at the pharmacy and Agnes with her job at the sewing factory. They usually would plan to spend most of their weekends seeing each other and if their schedules permitted would get a week day in if possible. They always communicated by phone. These young lovers agreed that they would never let too much time go by without touching base. For the next few months, things went as they planned.

Christmas 1962

This turned out to be a very special Christmas for Jack and Agnes. Jack started to visit Agnes's church. Jack was Baptist from southern Baptist roots. Agnes was Catholic. She invited him to come to the mid night mass with her. This was quite an experience for Jack. He enjoyed being in church with her even though he did not understand the rituals. He enjoyed sharing the mid night mass with her. She was very proud that Jack shared this experience with her.

Later on that Christmas morning Jack went to Agnes's house to have breakfast with her family. This was a very special treat.

Agnes's mom fixed a big pancake breakfast with country sausage and eggs. After breakfast, they exchanged gifts. Agnes and Jack went by Jack's house and exchanged gifts with his family. They were both so very happy. Agnes and Jack then visited her aunts and uncles. They exchanged gifts and just had such a wonderful time. They both had large families and by the time they got back to Agnes's house it was night time. This was indeed a very special Christmas because Jack saved his money to buy Agnes a special gift. He bought her a leopard skin coat that she admired one day when they were window shopping. Jack felt good that he was able to make her so happy. She was so kind and thoughtful and deserved anything he could give her.

CHAPTER SIX

...Growing Closer Together...

Spring 1963

This turned out to be a very special spring for Jack and Agnes. Jack had a brother that was not quite two years older than he was. His name was Freddie. Freddie was getting married and Jack was his best man. It so happened that Agnes was a maid in the wedding party. Everyone in Jack's family was very happy to see Freddie get married. Freddie was a little wild and they hoped having some responsibility would help to settle him down. Miss Louraine was especially happy to see him get married. This pleased Jack very much. Jack figured that when his time would come maybe she would take the same attitude. Jack and Agnes became even closer after participating in the wedding. They even let their guard down a couple of times when they engaged in sex. They knew they would get married, the question was when.

Jack and Agnes were enjoying the happiest time of their relationship when things took a one hundred and eighty degree turn. Jack visited Agnes one evening and she sat him down to talk with her. Agnes did not know quite how to tell Jack what she had to tell him or how to start. She simply said, "Jack, we have to talk." Without delaying the news any longer, she told Jack she was pregnant. Initially, Jack was stunned. He then said I'm going to be a father. Agnes said what are we going to do?. Jack paused for a moment and said we will get married. What about school? Jack told her he would cut back on his class load and it would take a little longer. Jack said he would ask his mother to sign for him because he would not be twenty one for four months. Agnes felt better after seeing how Jack responded to the news. She waited for Jack to talk with his mother.

Jack did not know how to approach his mother with the news. He informed her that he needed to talk to her. He asked her how she felt about Freddie's marriage. She was very pleased to see Freddie get married. Jack then said it looks like there will be another marriage in the near future. She looked at him with a puzzled look on her face and asked who? Jack smiled and said me. She responded, "Son, I don't have time to be joking around." Jack stopped smiling and said," I'm not joking." I need you to sign so that Agnes and I can get married. She asked what about your school. Can't you wait until you finish college. Jack said no, I can't wait that long. Why? His mother snapped. Because Agnes is pregnant. That's when Jack's mother lost it. Why that lying little tramp. She told me that the two you were not having sex. Did you have sex with her? How can you be sure that it's your baby. Stop it, Jack shouted. How can you say those horrible things about a wonderful girl like Agnes. I thought you really liked her. It ain't about her fool, it's you I care about. What about your future? I will continue to go to school Jack said. How in the world do you expect to get married, go to school and take care of a family on a drug store job? You big fool, you. Well, You won't have to worry about that, because "I ain't signing nothing." Jack could not believe his ears. He loved and respected his mother so much. He was devastated by the way she reacted. He did not know how he was going to break this news to Agnes. Jack's mother looked at him with total disgust as he turned and walked away.

Jack went to his room to be alone for awhile as he to tried to digest the conversation that just took place. After an hour, Jack decided to visit Agnes. When he arrived, he was not his usual happy go lucky or upbeat self. He did not have to say a word because Agnes took one look at him and knew that things did not go well. She just held out her arms and said come to me Jack. Jack told her that his mother was very disappointed and would not sign for him to get married. Jack did not have the heart to tell Agnes the awful things that his mother really said. Agnes looked at Jack and said, "We'll just have to wait." Agnes had not told any of her family members that she was pregnant. She wanted to work things out with Jack first. Jack did not want to wait too long because he knew how hard this would be on her. He told Agnes not to worry, he would continue to work on his mother. He also stated that if she still would not sign, he would ask his father to sign for him. Jack knew that this would be a long shot because his father and mother had been separated for years. He was very concerned about Agnes's condition and knew that she had not always been in the best of health. He wanted to do the worrying for both of them. He told her that he would talk to her soon.

The Sinister Plan

Little did Jack know what he was about to face. He did not have a clue or any knowledge of the terrible ordeal he was destined to experience. Jack returned home to talk with his mother again. He approached her very cautiously. She told him that she was very sorry that she exploded on him the way that she did. Jack listened intensely to her conversation. Mother informed her son that it was not his fault he was in this situation. She approached him and said, "Son, you have been taken advantage of"." Do you believe that I love you? "Yes", said Jack. You know I would do anything to protect you. "I believe that", Jack responded. Well, I'm going to protect you now. Jack told his mother he did not need any protection from Agnes. I love her and she loves me. I did not just meet Agnes, I've known her for a very long time. She's a very wonderful young woman. That's what I'm talking about replied Jack's mother. She has you thinking that. She has total control over you. You don't know very much about these types of things. What type of things? Jack was growing very impatient with his mother. Jack's mother implied that Agnes was evil and had cast some type of spell over him. Jack could not believe what he was hearing. I don't want to hear anymore talk like that he responded. Jack's mother could see that he was not responding the way she hoped he would. She would have his older brother speak to him.

Jack's mother returned with his oldest brother that he respected very much. He was a war hero and more of a surrogate father to his younger siblings She had already convinced Teddy(Jack's oldest brother) that Agnes was taking the advantage of Jack. Teddy was very diplomatic and explained to Jack that it was possible for some women to cast a spell on others to get them to do exactly as they wished. Jack told him that this was not true about Agnes. He looked his brother straight in his eyes and told him, "I trust Agnes with my life." That's just how much I love her. His mother then interrupted and said, "I told you he had it bad." We have to get him some help. Get who some help snapped Jack. What are you talking about?. Teddy told Jack to hold off on making any decisions for a couple of days and to refrain from seeing Agnes just for a day or so, He also asked him not to be in communication with her. This kind of talk had really frightened Jack and he agreed only to hold off for one day.

This was all the time that Jack's mother needed to go to phase two of her plan. She was convinced that nobody could be as perfect as Jack made Agnes out to be. She was going to do everything she possibly could to get him to see the light. She had already asked

Jack's sisters if they ever saw her with any other men. The older sisters saw this as an opportunity to please their mother. Even the most innocent situations were blown out of proportion. Besides, they thought they were protecting their younger brother. It was very easy for his mother to manipulate them. She believed in getting the entire family to stick together when she thought one was going astray. Jack's younger sister Carolyn was a very good friend of Agnes and felt that none of the malicious gossip was true. She knew Agnes was a decent person but was not in a position to speak out against the others.

By the time Jack's mom and brother(Teddy) had met with him again, phase two of her plan had taken shape. She was able to supply names of people that Agnes had supposedly slept with. A name on the list was that of Sammy. For the first time in the conversation, Jack was not one hundred percent sure this was not true. He thought back to the situation with Sammy. He did not say anything but listened for what was coming next. Jack's mother told him that she had discussed his situation with someone who was convinced that he was under some type of spell. Jack stated emphatically that he would not go to see anyone. Since Jack would not agree to go to this person they sent him something to take. Jack said he was not taking a darn thing. Jack's mother left the potion and asked his brother to talk to him. Teddy told Jack that he had more experience about certain things than he did and to trust him. Jack was so confused he did not know which way to turn. Teddy told him it was only one way for him to be sure. If Agnes was the type of person that they suspected her to be then the potion would break the spell. If it was not true than it would not have any effect. He convinced Jack that it would not harm him in any way. Jack knew within his heart that this stuff was not true about Agnes. It was no way she could be that great an actor to fool Jack into thinking she loved him that much. Jack just wanted to put this situation behind him. Teddy told Jack that he could not see or talk to Agnes while he took the potion. He also told Jack that he would have to get rid of everything that she gave him. The most precious thing he had was her high school picture. This was a beautiful portrait that sat on Jack's dresser. He told his brother that he could not part with that. Teddy told him that the only way the potion would work was to get rid of everything including the photograph. By this time Jack was so frightened, he stood by while Teddy disposed of the photograph. Teddy asked Jack to start taking the potion. Jack took one teaspoon and told Teddy that he was tired and wanted to get some sleep. A week had passed and Jack had not made any contact with Agnes. She had called the house numerous times but none of her calls were allowed to go through. Jack was just going to work and coming straight home. He had been convinced by people he loved and respected very much that he was in imminent danger. After the second week, Jack told Teddy he was not taking anymore of that crap and he wanted to see Agnes. He was being watched like a prisoner in his home. Teddy told Jack that maybe he had already taken enough to be free of the spell. He told Jack that he would walk with him pass Agnes's house. The next day Teddy and Jack went for a walk. As they approached Agnes's house they saw her sitting on the steps. When Agnes saw Jack she smiled and stood to her feet. Teddy told Jack to keep walking and don't look back. Jack took a few more steps and Agnes called out to him. Teddy told him to be strong and keep walking. Jack looked back and saw the tears streaming down Agnes's face. He continued to walk and he began to cry himself. When he got home he went straight to his room, took that bottle of whatever it was and slammed it against the wall. He started back out the door and Teddy grabbed him and pinned him against the wall. He was bigger and stronger than Jack, but Jack had reached his boiling point. When he saw the woman he loved in the kind of pain she was experiencing he knew that was it. He told Teddy that he was leaving. Teddy told him he was not. Jack loved and respected Teddy very much but he looked him in his eyes and told him he would have to kill him to keep him from going to the woman he loved. Teddy had been through a war and had experienced a lot but when he saw the tears stream down his younger brother's face this was too much. He had not witnessed that type of determination since he was a prisoner of war trying to get back home. He looked at his little brother and said, "Okay, I'm through with it." Do what you have to little brother.

Jack walked right pass him, down his steps and out the door. He headed straight for Agnes's house. When he reached the corner he saw Agnes's mother. He asked her where was Agnes. She said

Agnes was at home crying her eyes out. She said she would not tell her anything. I was coming to see you so you could tell me what was going on. Jack told Miss Helen that Agnes needed him and he was going to her now. He left Miss Helen standing on the corner and started to run toward Agnes's house. When he got to Agnes's house he called out for her. She came to the door tears still coming down her face. Agnes I love, I love you, please forgive me. They embraced, both of them crying. Agnes told Jack she did not know what to think when her calls would not go through. Jack said it was a long story. Then, you walked pass me. That was just too much for me to handle. Jack told her he was just so sorry he put her through this ordeal. Agnes said," Jack I know it was not your doing." I have no doubt about your love for me. I just know you must have been going through some difficult times. Jack said, "Baby, if you only knew." He was too embarrassed to tell her what actually happened. He told Agnes that he would ask his father to sign so they could get married.

The next day Jack visited with his father and told him his situation. Jack's father told him that he thought he was being very responsible and was doing the right thing. Jack said," Dad, I'm doing the only thing I can". I love her with all my heart and soul. Jack's father said he would do anything for him, but he did not want to go against his mother's wishes. He explained to Jack that he had not been a part of his life for some time and he did not feel he had the right to sign for him now. I hope you understand, Jack. He appreciated his father being honest with him. He also understood the situation he would put his father in.

Jack told Agnes of his father's decision not to sign for him. They both understood and went on to plan two. Jack stated he only had a couple of months before he would be twenty one and could sign for himself. Agnes was feeling so much better now that she was assured that Jack would stand by her. She told Jack that she admired his courage. She knew how much Jack's mother meant to him and for him to make a decision against her wishes took extraordinary courage. She felt really blessed to be loved by a man like this. Agnes also knew that Jack's mother said some terrible things about her that were not true but she chose not to address this issue. Agnes understood that Jack's mom wanted to do what she felt was best for her son. Miss Louraine wanted her son to complete his education uninterrupted. She knew Jack had a lot potential. Agnes loved Jack and respected his mother. She also knew how much Jack loved his mother and to say or do anything to take away from that would be counter productive. Jack would not blame her if she was bitter with his family. Remarkably, Agnes was just the opposite. In spite of the dastardly treatment she received by Jack's family, she did not speak ill of them. Jack told Agnes that she was truly one remarkable person. She was really an earth angel. They had come to grips with the fact that they would have to wait just alittle longer to be married.

Jack and Agnes had just witnessed the worst nightmare of their young lives. It would leave a scar on them for years to come. Agnes would fare much better than Jack in coping with the situation. She was a person with tremendous faith and possessed that special quality that allowed her to forgive her trangressors and move on with her life. But, Jack on the other hand would not fair as well. Because of the love and respect he had for his mother he did not want to believe she was capable of such treachery. This experience left Jack devastated. He was very depressed and suffered from constant headaches. His relationship with his mother had suffered irreparable harm. He thought long and hard what he would say when he talked with her. He prayed for guidance. Ironically, it was his mother who taught him how to pray. She also taught him how to be a good judge of character in people. Jack thought about all the good things she had done for him and how hard she worked to keep her family together. He loved his mother more than anything in this world and tried very hard to please her.

This is why it was so difficult to face her after this ordeal, but face her he must.

Jack told his mother that he needed to talk with her. He stated he did not want to get into any type of argument but needed to clear the air. Jack's mother did not oppose the meeting that Jack wanted to have with her. She could see that he was hurting badly and wanted him to know that in spite of their differences, she loved him none the less. Jack told his mother that he loved her with all his heart and soul. He could understand why she was upset with him for putting school on hold to do something she felt he was ill prepared to do. Jack knew she would not be happy with his decision to get married and start a family. This was an awesome responsibility even for people older and much more experienced than Jack.

Jack explained to his mother that he had been seeing Agnes for over five years. She helped him to remain focused on his goal to complete his college education. She was instrumental in them not having sex until this year. Jack wanted his mother to know that it was he who pressured Agnes for sex. She always managed to keep him under control when it came to sex. She finally gave in when she felt their relatioship was about to end. I want you to know that she was and is a decent human being that I love and cherish very much. It is because she is such a good person with very high morals and standards that I wish to save her any embarassment by marrying her now as opposed to later. It has never been a question in my mind if I would marry her, but when I would do it.

Jack looked at his mother and said the question I have to ask of you is why did you go to such lengths to try to destroy her? Do you really think that Agnes is the type of person that could do all those horrible things you accused her of doing? Do you think that I am so naive that I would not know what true love is? Jack's mother did not answer him but remained silent and subdued during the entire conversation. Jack was very careful not to raise his voice while he talked to his mother. He spoke to her with respect. He was looking for some answers. Miss Louraine did not have any answers for him and was careful not to say anything to make a bad situation worst. She did not want to lose her son completely.

CHAPTER SEVEN

...Wedding Plans

Jack and Agnes started making their wedding plans. Jack told Agnes not to expect any help from his family. Agnes was so very perceptive and could see that Jack was really hurting. She informed Jack that her family had offered to help them any way they could. Her godmother who was also her aunt had offered her house to have the wedding reception. Her aunts and older sisters would be responsible for coordinating and preparing food for the reception. They would be married in the Catholic church that Agnes attended. Jack was not Catholic, but agreed to attend the classes in preparation for the wedding. Jack knew how important this was to Agnes. Agnes wanted Jack to help her with the wedding invitations. She asked him to prepare a list of his friends and relatives. Jack told Agnes he did not see why he should include his family after what they had put them through. Jack then confessed to Agnes that he had a run in with one of his older sisters that paid him a visit in the drug store. She told him that they (his family) would not help with the wedding. Jack became angry and told her that we don't need your help. He then said he did not care if he ever saw or heard from any of them again. She cried and ran from the store. Jack said he was very sorry he said that but he was very hurt. Agnes looked at him and caressed him. She said, "Jack, I know this is going to be difficult for you but you must put this behind you." Now help me with the list of names and addresses of your relatives. Jack looked at Agnes and told her she was one remarkable human being. That's why I love you so much. Agnes was concerned about Jack and knew she had to help him get through this crisis.

The Wedding Day Approaches

The wedding day was only a few weeks away and Jack spent most of his time being very attentive to Agnes. When he was not there, he was with his best man(James). If ever there was a time he needed a friend it was now. James was very concerned about Jack also. He would talk with him and ask how he was holding up under the pressure. Jack confided in James, but there were things that happened that he would not even share with him. James kept a watchful eye on his buddy. He knew how close Jack was to his family and how much he loved Agnes. James knew that this was ripping Jack apart.

Jack tried very hard to mask his feelings, but anyone that knew him well enough could tell there was something bothering him very deeply. Jack never thought he would have to choose between Agnes and his family. When faced with that ultimatum, he chose to be with Agnes. He was prepared to divorce himself from his family if it became necessary. This proved to be much harder than Jack ever imagined. He knew he had made the right decision, but it left a void in his life. He especially missed the closeness he shared with his mother. Jack was well aware that their relationship would never be the same. Jack had assumed a defensive attitude when it came to Agnes. He was now very protective of her.

Agnes suffered from morning sickness a lot and at times became very ill. This really upset Jack, but there was not much he could do about it. Agnes was very perceptive and pretended she was alright when Jack was around. That's how she was. Always concerned about someone else and their feelings. She was the type of indvidual that avoided confrontations, very fair minded and considered by all that knew her to be a peace maker.

This is why Agnes chose not to exclude Jack's family from the wedding. She obtained the information from Jack and made sure the invitations were sent out. She kept Jack informed of all of her actions. Jack was obviously pleased, but under the circumstances he would not blame Agnes if she chose to do otherwise. Jack realized that he was blessed to have someone like Agnes in his life. The love they shared gave him the courage to face life with whatever setbacks or obstacles they had to encounter.

As the wedding day approached, reality began to set in with Jack's family. He sensed that the opposition and the mood had softened. Although he remained distanced, he was tuned into what was going on in his family. He was very careful not to let his guard down again. After going through probably the worst experience of his life he was cautious not to be vulnerable again. The only family member that he opened up to a little was Carolyn. The sister that was a close friend to Agnes.

Jack was the type of person that would give his all if you were close to him. Once he was hurt or felt betrayed he would close up like a clam. His family was well aware of this fact, especially his mom. Jack's mother loved and protected all of her children. She was very possessive and would go to any extreme to protect them. When it came to the ones she loved, she had the ferocity of a lioness protecting her cubs. She also knew her children very well and could read them like a book. She knew how Jack was and if he felt he had been wronged, she could lose him forever.

Jack and his mother were not talking very much these days, but she knew that she could not let him leave with the distance that was now between them. The plans for the wedding were all set and things were beginning to fall in place. Agnes's family(her sisters and aunt's) played a major role in coordinating and assigning responsibilities for the reception.

Jack and Agnes obviously very much in love, were very practical and knew they needed to plan beyond the wedding day. Under the circumstances, they knew they were not prepared to just jump out and handle all the expenses associated with married life. Agnes informed

Jack that they could stay with her family until they were able to secure housing on their own. Jack had been very thrifty and had managed to save enough money for next year's college tuition and fees. With the baby coming, Jack knew he would have to tap into these funds to pay for Agnes's medical expenses. Jack had always been very independent and he accepted the responsibility for caring for Agnes and his unborn child.

Easing the Tension

With the wedding only a week away, Jack's mother realized that she needed to make sure that she left open a line of communication with her son. She approached Jack and told him that there were some things that she needed to discuss with him. She told Jack that even though she did not approve of him getting married, she knew it was a reality and wanted to give him her blessing. She also asked Jack if he had given any thought to where he and Agnes would live. Jack was very quiet as he listened to his mother. He then responded saying that he and Agnes would be staying with her parents for awhile. Jack's mother did not respond to this statement. She informed Jack that she had a friend that lived alone in a large house and wanted to rent a small apartment to a young couple. The lady was a retired nurse and a widow. She did not have any children and was not looking for much rent. Jack's mom was not expecting an answer right away but wanted him to discuss it with Agnes.

Jack did discuss it with Agnes and asked her for her opinion. She told Jack that she would be okay with whatever decision he made. Jack told Agnes before he made a decision he thought they should meet with the lady and look at the apartment. Jack and Agnes decided to meet with her. The lady's name was Mrs Wheeler. She was a retired nurse that lived alone. She seemed to be very friendly and very lonlely. Mrs Wheeler showed Jack and Agnes the apartment. After having a lengthly conversation with the couple, she asked them if they would come to live with her. She forgot to mention anything about the rent. When Jack asked about the rent, he was very surprised how reasonable it was. Jack told her he and Agnes would discuss the matter and give her an answer the next day.

Jack and Agnes decided to take the apartment. It was small but affordable. Besides, Agnes was tuned in to a lot of things going on with Jack. She knew he would rather be on their own if at all possible. Jack also appreciated the fact that Mrs Wheeler was a nurse. He felt she would be good company to Agnes considering her condition. They called Mrs Wheeler and told her they would take the apartment. Agnes reminded Jack to call his mother and thank her for sharing this information with them. They both knew she was trying to break the ice and show she was concerned about them. She also wanted to make sure she did not close the door completely on their relationship. This was also a relief to Jack. While he was very fond of Agnes's family, he wanted to live alone with his new bride.

Wedding Day

Jack and Agnes could not wait until they were married. Now that the day had come they both were very nervous. Jack had just reached the age of twenty one and Agnes was nineteen. Jack turned twenty one five days before the wedding. He was able to sign for his marriage license himself. He was very proud of that fact. The young couple was married on a Saturday in July. The weather was very nice and the church was filled to capacity. They were married in the Catholic church that Agnes attended. It was a very lovely ceremony.

Jack was more nervous than Agnes. Half way through the marriage ceremony as they were kneeling, Jack could not stop his legs from shaking. The ceremony was actually not that long, but to Jack it seemed like an eternity. After exchanging wedding vows, the married couple mingled with friends, relatives and well wishers. Everyone was very happy for the newly weds and felt they truly deserved each other. They were such a beautiful couple. Both families were united and the joy resignated through the church. One would never know that any tension ever existed. This was truly a blessed occasion.

Reception

Everyone left the churh at midday and headed for the wedding reception hosted by Agnes's aunt. She was also her godmother. The reception was at the aunt's house. Tables were set up in the back yard. The grills were fired up and the food was very tasty. Agnes's brother worked at a bakery and baked the wedding cake for the couple. Everything was coordinated so well. The reception went on for hours late into the evening. Jack and Agnes were very tired but also very happy. They were pleased that everyone had such a nice time.

Jack and Agnes received many gifts. Practically everything they needed to get started was among the gifts. They also received many envelopes stuffed with cash. Friends and relatives knew they could use the cash. It could not come at a better time. Agnes was now three months pregnant and could no longer work. They spent their wedding night at her parents' house.

CHAPTER EIGHT

...Facing Life as a Married Couple

Settling in the new apartment

The next morning the young couple moved into their new apartment. They only took their clothes and some personal items. The small apartment was furnished and Jack and Agnes had the use of a large kitchen. Mrs Wheeler was very happy to see them moving in. She needed the company as much as the couple needed the apartment.

In the ensuing weeks, Jack would come home from work to find the ladies engaged in conversation and bonding very well. Agnes wanted to stop and fix Jack's food but Jack insisted that she continue with her conversation. He appreciated the fact that Agnes had someone to talk to and monitor her condition. M's Wheeler often discussed with the couple how she wanted to help Agnes care for the child when it comes. She had no relatives in the area and only a nephew and his wife that lived out of town. She never received any visitors, and the couple was like family to her.

Jack and Agnes were aware of the attachment M's Wheeler had to them. They knew they would need more space when the baby was born. Jack informed Agnes that the Department of Housing had recently completed a new devlopment in West Baltimore. They wanted to place an application so they could get on the waiting list. By the time they would be interviewed the baby would be here. The location would be perfect for them. They would be near their families and most of their friends. They completed an application and sent it in.

Meanwhile, M's Wheeler kept a watchful eye on Agnes while Jack was working. It was now September, and Jack registered for the fall semester for college. Because of the expenses associated with having a family, Jack was only able to take a couple of classes. He supplemented his income by driving a taxicab. Agnes was so proud of Jack and wished she could contribute more on the financial end. She was having difficulty with the pregnancy and had to stop working at the sewing factory. Jack assured her that all was well and not to worry about such things. He always comforted her and told her that if he needed to work extra jobs to make ends meet that was okay. Jack really enjoyed being the provider and he was always very thrifty and managed the finances well.

It was now mid October of 1963 when a letter came from the housing authority. Jack got in from work late that evening when

Agnes approached him with some good news. They received a letter advising them of an interview date for public housing. They were both very happy, then momentarily the happiness was replaced with sadness. If they were accepted for housing, they did not know how they would break the news to Mrs Wheeler. She had become very attached to them for the short time they had been living with her.

Jack and Agnes kept the interview appointment. They took all the required documents. The interview went very well. They were informed that they met all the criteria including income requirements. They were eligible for public housing. All that was left was for them to pass the back ground and reference check. They also entered their preference for the newly completed Murphy Homes. They returned home after the interview feeling very confident. After talking it over between themselves, they agreed that they needed to discuss the possibility of moving with Mrs Wheeler.

Jack and Agnes approached Mrs Wheeler and told her there was something they need to discuss with her. They informed her that they placed an application with public housing because of the additional room that would be needed for the baby. She was told that they had an interview with housing and would be hearing from them sometime in the future. M's Wheeler was very quiet and subdued as she got the news. She was just getting used to having the young people around. Initially, she thought it was something she did to make them want to move.

They assured her that she was the most loving and caring landlady that anyone could hope for. Jack and Agnes informed her that she was like family. They explained to her that the apartment was very nice but just too small with the baby coming. They knew they would need more space.

Agnes told Mrs Wheeler she certainly could not do any more to make them feel like a part of her family. Jack informed her that they had an opportunity to get into the new developement that was just built. M's Wheeler shared with the couple that she was looking forward to helping Agnes care for the baby. Agnes assured her that when the baby comes she will get an opportunity to spend plenty of time at her house. Mrs Wheeler began to smile and felt much better after hearing that reassurance.

Tragedy Strikes

It was the 22nd day of November, 1963. Jack and Agnes were preparing to have Thanksgiving with their family and friends. Jack decided to get a haircut at the neighborhood barber shop. It was mid morning and Jack was in the barber's chair finishing up his hair cut when he heard over the TV the most horrible news of his life. The announcer had cut into the program with a bulletin stating that President John F. Kennedy had just been shot in Dallas, Texas. Jack could not believe what he was hearing. He quickly paid the barber and ran to his apartment. When he arrived he rushed to tell Agnes what had happened. They turned on the T.V. and heard the news again. By this time, Walter Conkrite had announced that the president was dead. This was a very sad and tragic occasion. This was indeed like losing a member of the family. This was a very popular president with a very young family. Jack and Agnes often talked about this president and stated that he would be the first president they would get a chance to vote for. Jack had just reached voting age and was not old enough to vote for him when he ran for office in 1960. This was indeed a very sad time for the country.

Two weeks later, Jack and Agnes got the news they were waiting for. They received notification from the Housing Authority to bring the requested documents and sign their lease. They were accepted into the newly constructed Murphy homes. Upon signing the lease and paying the required fees, Jack and Agnes were given their keys and a move in date.

The young couple was very happy to share the good news with their family. Jack's brother and his wife also received a letter from Housing stating that they were accepted in the same building. They both had move in dates for the first of December. Both apartments were located on the 13th. floor with just a coulpe of apartments separating them. In the same building a few floors below Jack and Agnes, Agnes's brother and his wife had an apartment. This turned out to be a very good arrangement because Agnes was only a month away from her due date. Jack's brother and his wife had a 3 month old baby girl. There was a very good support system in the same building with close relatives in the same unit.

Both Jack and Agnes's families lived only a short distance from the new Homes.

They also enjoyed their view from the 13th. floor calling it their penthouse apartment. Jack enjoyed taking photographs of the city from his apartment. Jack and Agnes while being surrounded by family and friends did not spend much time visiting other apartments. They preferred each others company. They spent much of their time listening to jazz albums and talking to each other.

Jack was still employed at the drug store and drove a taxi on evenings and weekends. He had put away enough money to handle the present medical expenses, but realized that he needed to find a job that had benefits. He submitted applications throughout the area.

Approaching due date

It is now the second week in December and Agnes is very much pregnant and always uncomfortable. Jack did everything he could to make her comfortable. Agnes could not find a comfortable position to rest. She got very little rest and became very irritable. Jack was constantly catering to her and always managed to get a smile out of her. He knew she was very miserable, but tried to help her keep her sense of humor. He always managed to bring the things she liked to eat when he came home late at night. There were times when he would get up late at night to go out and pick up chinese food if she so desired. He pampered Agnes very much and enjoyed doing it. He told her that she was his special angel and there was nothing he wouldn't do for her. When Jack told her this, Agnes would look at him and smile with her approval. This would take her mind off the miserable feelings she had to endure.

Christmas was only a couple of days away and Agnes stayed off her feet as much as possible. Her sister (Sandy) would visit her during the day and would often stay until Jack came home from work. This was the first Christmas that Jack and Agnes would spend as a married couple. Jack took Agnes to visit with her family and then returned to spend a quiet evening at their apartment doing what they like to do most, holding each other and listening to music. The baby was due between Christmas and New Year's Day. At the time, Jack and Agnes was hoping that the baby would be born on Christmas Day. Christmas had come and gone, and it was obvious that Jack and Agnes would not get their wish.

The weather had changed drastically between Christmas and the New year. The young couple spent a quiet New Year's Eve at their apartment. Jack got up early New Year's day and fixed breakfast. He was scheduled to work at the drug store. Weather conditions deteriorated and driving was hazardous. Jack wanted to get an early start. Agnes kept going to the bath room and Jack was getting worried about her. He did not want to leave her by herself and asked her to come with him. He dropped her off at his mother's house to spend the day with his sister. He was very careful with her because there was ice and sleet that covered the street and pavement. He helped her up the marble steps that were covered with ice. Agnes felt that Jack was making too much fuss over her, but really appreciated his concern. This turned out to be a very wise decision on Jack's part. Jack could see his mother's house from the drug store.

Jack was not at work two hours before he got a call from his sister. She told Jack that Agnes had gone into labor and his brother was taking her to the hospital. At that moment, Jack looked out of the store window and saw his brother coming down the steps with Agnes. Jack rushed to the back of the pharmacy to tell Doc what was going on. Doc told Jack to be very careful driving in this weather and he would call James to cover for him.

The hospital was not very far away. By the time Jack left the store, Agnes and his brother were already at the hospital. When Jack arrived at the hospital he was informed by the nurse that Agnes's water broke and and she was in the delivery room. Within a short time the baby was born. Jack soon found out that he was the proud father of a 7 pound 14oz. baby girl. Jack was very happy to hear the good news and was very eager to find out how his wife was doing. The doctor told Jack that the baby and mother were both doing fine. Soon, Jack got to see his wife and baby girl. He telephoned Agnes's family and gave them the good news. Agnes's sister(Sandy) was very excited about the birth of her niece.

Then the fact hit Jack that he and Agnes had a baby born on New Year's Day. Everyone felt very close to this baby. But no one felt as close as Agnes and Jack, considering the ordeal that they both went through. This child was literally smothered with love from day one. Jack could not wait to take his family home. For the first month, Jack did everything for the baby. He just wanted Agnes to rest and to regain her strength. Sandy was at the apartment a lot and often had to compete with Jack to see who would hold the baby. She began to visit her sister while Jack was working so she could have the baby to herself.

Jack and Agnes visited her parents frequently. Jack felt very comfortable around Agnes' family. Jack and his in-laws had a very good relationship. Agnes and Jack had a great relationship and she knew he enjoyed being around her family. Although Jack was enjoying himself, Agnes knew something was bothering him. When they were alone, Agnes approached Jack and said let's talk. She asked Jack when was he going to take the baby pass his mother's house. He would always reply, "soon". Agnes was very perceptive and knew that this was a touchy subject for Jack. She healed more rapidly from the ordeal with Jack's mother than he did. Jack tried to mask his feelings but was still bothered by that experience.

Agnes held Jack as tears filled his eyes. He found it very hard to express just what he was feeling. He loved his mother very much but found it difficult to be around her with his family. When he would visit, he was always alone. She would always ask where was the baby and he always had an excuse. Jack felt very protective of Agnes and little Veronica. Agnes was very good for Jack and would help him to cope with the situation. She was the only one he would talk to concerning his problems. Jack was very good at hiding his pain from everyone except Agnes. She told him he must try to get over his pain and move on. She knew it was not going to be easy for him but always tried to help him. She knew he loved his mother very much and his mother loved him very much.

One day Jack came home from work and found a note from Agnes.[Jack pick me and the baby up from your mother's house after you eat. Your food is in the oven.] Jack had his dinner and went to his mother's house. Agnes and Veronica had spent the day with Jack's sister(Carolyn) and Jack's mother. When Jack arrived he saw his mother holding Veronica and singing to her. Jack looked at Agnes and smiled. After spending some time at his mother's house, he took his family home.

The young couple put their baby to bed and had their quiet time. Jack held Agnes and told her she was just too good to be true. As much as Jack wanted to take his baby to his mother's house he could not bring himself to do it. He told Agnes she was truly an angel sent from heaven. I love you so very much. You are just too good for this earth. You knew just what was bothering me and what was needed to start the healing process. She looked at Jack and said "I pray to GOD everyday and ask for his guidance and he always direct me." With that statement, they began to pray together and held each other for a while. More and more Jack realized how blessed he was to have this wonderful human being by his side.

The Healing Process

Jack and Agnes got a lot of pleasure watching little Veronica develop and grow. They spent much of their time enjoying each other. Jack could not wait to get off from work to rush home to be with his family. He and Agnes spent much of their time quietly listening to music and talking. At times, Jack would sit quietly reading or playing his jazz albums. This had a therapeutic effect on Jack. Their were many things on his mind and music helped to sort them out.

Jack often thought about how close he came to losing Agnes, and the terrible ordeal that she had to go through. He blamed himself for not standing up and taking action sooner. Agnes always seemed to be tuned in when he was feeling down. She always told him not to blame himself for others actions. She knew how much Jack loved his mother and how much his mother loved him. Agnes told Jack that his mother did what she thought was best for her son. Jack would look at Agnes in disbelief, and would tell her over and over that she was an angel sent from God. He would tell her that she was so kind and forgiving. Jack tried his best to put this thing behind him, but had no idea the lasting effect it had on him and his family.

CHAPTER NINE

...Growing Responsibilities...

There were other things on Jack's mind as well. Agnes was not in the best of health and Jack knew he had to provide for his family's financial needs as well as their medical needs. He submitted numerous applications for jobs that provided health benefits. Jack also knew he would not be able to go to school fulltime. Because of the negative experience Jack and Agnes received from his family, he became very protective of his family. They received a lot of support from Agnes's family and as a result spent the majority of their free time with Agnes's family. It was not that Jack didn't care for his family, but because he cared so much it was too painful for him to be around them. Jack missed out on many of his family's functions. All of his siblings were probably not aware of the ordeal that Jack and Agnes suffered. Ironically, it was through Agnes's prodding that Jack made as many functions as he did.

Jack interviewed for a few jobs and accepted a job with a well known steel plant that had excellent benefits and paid a good salary.

This job came at the right time, because Agnes informed Jack that she was pregnant with their second child. The job Jack accepted required that he work a swing shift. This prevented Jack from going to school the next semester. After working on this job for a few months, Jack was able to work a single shift. The only shift available on a permanent basis was the 11pm. to7am. shift. Jack jumped at this opportunity because he was able to take some courses toward his college degree. Jack was determined, no matter how long it took him he would obtain his degree.

Jack was also motivated because once he obtained his degree he would be able to get the kind of job he wanted with the state or local government. Jack always placed his name on the personnel list for city and state jobs. In his spare time, he went to civil service and completed applications for everything he felt he was qualified for and some things he knew he was not qualified for.

Jack also managed to save a little money. He informed housing management of the change in his income and the need for a larger apartment. After discussing his situation with the housing manager, the manager informed him that there were no larger units available now, but he would be placed on the waiting list. Jack also discussed the fact that he was trying to complete college and provide for a family. The housing manager was impressed by Jack's drive and determination and informed him that he would not raise his rent at this time. It gave Jack an opportunity to save even more money.

Jack saw a house in the paper and felt this would be perfect for a growing family. It stated that you could buy it like rent and would not require a down payment. Jack took Agnes to look at the house to see if it would meet her approval. Agnes liked the house, but with her not being able to work felt it was probably too much for Jack. She did not want to hurt Jack's feeling or discourage him because he wanted to do so much. The house had hard wood floors, a finished basement and a nice fenced yard. It also had three bedrooms. This house seemed perfect for Jack's family. Jack put in his bid for the house and was soon notified that he met all the landlord's requirements and could have the house.

Jack took the money he saved for school and moved his family in the house. For the next six months, Jack and Agnes really enjoyed their little house. After the second child was born, the expenses began to mount. Jack was becoming disatisfied with his job at the steel plant. The job had excellant benefits and paid a decent wage, but offered no future for Jack. The job was hard and dirty and Jack felt he could do better. He also let another semester go by without getting back to school. Jack continued to place applications everywhere he could think of.

When he came in one morning from his job at the steel mill, there was a letter for him. It was a response from one of the applications he sent out. Jack followed up with an interview and found out the job was at a chemical plant. Jack was a chemistry major before he switched his major to sociology. He did well on the interview and discussed the job offer with Agnes. She encouraged Jack to do whatever would make him satisfied. Jack decided to take the job.

The job was a chemical operator's helper. It paid about the same as the job at the steel mill with similar benefits. The only down side was the job was also a swing job requiring an employee to work three shifts. Jack took the job so he could get away from the steel plant. He knew he would not be able to attend school for awhile but he knew he needed a job that would be adequate for him to take care of his family.

Jack was now adjusting to the responsibilities of a growing family. After three or four months on the job, Jack was promoted to a chemical operator. His salary had increased considerably. The extra money could not have come at a better time with Agnes not able to work at this time.

Things went well for a few months, then the expenses of maintaining a household began to rise. The mortgage or(rent payments) changed and Jack soon found out about the hidden expenses in maintaining a home. Jack also found out that he was not really buying the house but had entered a contract or ninety nine year lease that stated he could buy like rent. This was a new financing tool that unscrupulous landlords used to dupe unknowledgeable clients into thinking they were actually buying a home when they were really renting it. What this really did was to transfer all the expenses of maintaining the house to the occupant, while the landlord reaped the benefits of ownership.

With the birth of the second child, the expenses began to rise even more and Jack was feeling the pressure. Agnes was quite aware of what was going on and was always there to comfort Jack and offer her support. She was a very good manager and kept the spending at a minimum. She used her skills in dressmaking to make clothes for the family and needed repairs. Jack knew it would be awhile before Agnes could return to the work force and really preferred that she be at home while the children were young. This meant that Jack would have to increase the family's income by finding a second job.

Second Job

After checking the want adds, Jack applied for a couple of jobs that he thought would meet his needs without any major changes in his routine. There were a number of jobs that were available under the position of security guard. Jack applied for one and felt that this would serve his present needs. This was at a meat packing plant. The plant manager met with Jack and explained that they were looking for someone that would only be needed from mid-night to 7:00am. They needed someone on the night shift to patrol the plant grounds and to keep a watchful eye on the trailers that were packed with the various cuts of meat. Recently, trailers were broken into and the meat products were stolen. The manager also suspected that some employees were pilfering meat from the plant. The plant supervisor suspected that this was happening on the second shift. Most of those employees completed their work between 1:00am and 1:30am. The plant supervisors left by 11pm. The hours were perfect for Jack. He decided that he would accept the job.

Jack patrolled the plant regularly during his shift. His first two hours of his shift were primarily confined to patrolling the area of the plant where the employees were working. The employees in the plant noticed that Jack was very observant and business like. He was careful not to engage in too much conversation with the employees. He was polite, but very thorough. He did not become too familiar with the employees, but made his rounds making sure that everything was okay. One night while Jack was patrolling the plant he noticed something out of the ordinary. He saw one employee make a couple of trips to a 55 gallon steel drum and drop a package in it. When the employee noticed Jack he stopped and pulled out a cigarette as if to take a cigarette break. Jack just waved and continued to make his rounds. Jack doubled back very quickly and saw the employee going through the steel drum again. This time he did not see Jack. Jack shone his flash light on the employee and the steel drum. Jack asked what was going on. The employee was very nervous. Jack looked in the barrel and shone the light on the package. He asked the employee again, "What's going on". The young man confessed to Jack that he only picked out a few pieces of meat to take home with him. He told Jack it is not the prime cuts but only some inexpensive cuts of meat. He did not think the company would miss it.

Jack started writing down the employee's badge number and what he observed. The guy pleaded with Jack not to turn him in. He told Jack he had a large family and was only making minimum wage at the plant. The employee was not a meat cutter but a helper. He also told Jack his wife had just had a new born baby and things were very difficult now. The young man told Jack he could not afford to lose his job. He asked Jack to give him another chance.

At that time, Jack thought about his own situation and the struggle he was having taking care of a family. Jack thought over the situation and told the employee to put the items back and don't let it happen again. Jack did not want to see the guy lose his job over a few pieces of meat.

Things were going very well on the second job. Three or four weeks later, the plant supervisor approached Jack and told him he was very satisfied with his work. He also mentioned to Jack that there were no trailers broken into on his watch and the plant seems to be in order.

A few more weeks went by and all was well on the second job. One night when Jack arrived on the job, the same young man that Jack had saved from losing his job asked Jack if he had a lug wrench. He explained to Jack that one of the tires on his old car had a slow leak and he wanted to change the tire. He had a jack, but no lug wrench. Jack told him that he had a lug wrench that he could use but could not stop to get it for him. Jack was eager to start making his rounds. He gave the young man his trunk key and told him where he could find his lug wrench. About thirty minutes later, the man found Jack, thanked him and returned his trunk key.

The next morning after arriving at his home, Jack noticed that his lug wrench was on the back seat of his car. Jack shook his head in disgust and returned the lug wrench to the trunk. When he opened his trunk, he noticed a plastic bag that was not there before. Jack opened the bag and saw some cuts of meat in the bag. A pork shoulder, a few cuts of steaks and a round roast. Jack's first thought was to take the meat back to the plant but he would be late for his regular job. He barely had enough time to shower and eat breakfast. Jack also figured that returning the meat would cause more trouble than it was worth. He did not want to explain how the meat got in his trunk in the first place. Jack decided to keep the meat and put it in his freezer. The next night when Jack arrived at work he began checking all the trailers to make sure they were locked.

When Jack saw the employee who put the meat in his trunk, he began to talk to him. He asked him point blank why he put the meat in his trunk. The employee told Jack he just wanted to show his appreciation. Jack told the employee that you don't show it by jeopardizing your job and mine. Jack told the young man the only reason he did not return the meat was the problems it would cause. The young man accepted Jack's explanation and told him he was some piece of work. Jack told the young man to watch his step and to be thankful for the job he did have and to do everything he could to protect it.

Jack kept his job as a guard for a few more months. He managed to save some money and to catch up on his expenses. Jack had not lost sight of his goal, which was to return to school to complete his education.

Agnes was a very practical person with a lot of insight. She knew that Jack was under a lot of pressure. He was trying to maintain a home, provide for his family and return to school. Once Jack explained to Agnes the conditions of buying like rent, Agnes was ready to give up the house for a less expensive unit. Initially, Jack was opposed to this because he did not want to appear a failure or to have others think he could not care for his family. Jack was very proud and independent and certainly would not go to anyone in his family for advice or help. Agnes knew that the only way Jack was going to reach his objectives was to face the reality of giving up the house they were only renting and cutting expenses.

Agnes was not able to work yet because of poor health and very young children. Jack also preferred that she stay with the children while they were young. On this point they both agreed.

The house often became a point of friction between Jack and Agnes but Agnes was determined to help Jack through this crisis in spite of himself. Agnes loved Jack as much as Jack loved her and she had invested so much into their relationship. Jack always knew that Agnes had a very strong will and to some degree was very stubborn. One evening after dinner, Agnes wanted to talk about their situation. She tried to make Jack understand the difficulty of reaching his objectives while trying to hold onto the house with its mounting expenses. Jack became very irritated and said some very harsh things to Agnes about being lazy and wasteful. After saying those nasty things to his wife, Jack stormed out of the house. He went to a bar and had a few drinks. Normally, when Jack did indulge it was in the company of his friends in his home or their homes. He often enjoyed the company of his brothers-in law or his father-in-law. It was generally a family affair or a party when he did drink. This particular night Jack drank too much and could not remember where he parked his car when he left the bar. He had the good sense to return to the bar and have the bartender call him a cab. Ironically, when he got in the cab he gave his mother's address as his home. He paid the cab driver and proceeded up the steps of his old house. Jack tried his key in the door, when it did not fit he rang the door bell. His mother opened the door and could see that he had been drinking. Jack looked very supprised to see her. After realizing the blunder he made, he told his mother that he and Agnes had an argument The next thing he realized was being in his old room in the bed.

After sleeping for a couple of hours, Jack woke up and recognized where he was. He was very embarrased to find himself at his mother's house and did not care to face any of his family at this time. He decided to leave quietly before anyone got up. He rushed home after remembering where he parked his car the night before. When he got home, Agnes was sitting on a couch in the living room. He looked at her and told her how very sorry he was.

She told him she was very concerned about him. Agnes told Jack how much she loved and needed him and how she hurt when he was hurting. Jack looked at Agnes and confessed his love for her. He apologised for the things he said to her. He told her he was blessed to have such a loving and caring person in his life. Agnes informed Jack that his mother called to let her know that he was there. She was relieved to know that he was there and not any place where harm could come to him. Jack told Agnes that he did not know why he went to his mother's house of all places. Agnes stopped Jack and told him it was as natural as breathing for him to go to a home where he grew up and was obviously still loved very much. Jack looked at Agnes and told her she was wise beyond her years. She was always there to comfort him and to say the right things. She informed Jack that he was a very special individual with a lot of potenial and ambition. Jack she replied, "Don't be so hard on yourself." Jack told Agnes she was truly his angel. He listened to Agnes and they decided that in order for Jack to stay focused on all the things they wished to accomplish it was best to find a home more affordable.

Relocating

While visiting her mother one day, Agnes noticed a house with large apartments about two blocks away. She saw the signs out and copied down the information. She had a good feeling about this apartment building. She called Jack at work and asked him to pick her up at her mother's house. When Jack arrived, Miss Helen had his food ready for him. Jack's father-in-law said even he did not get that kind of treatment. Miss Helen a lady of few words responded that Jack was special. Jack smiled and had his dinner. When Jack and Agnes left with their daughters, Agnes asked Jack to pass by the apartments. Jack saw a very large house that had just been renovated. He asked Agnes to copy down the information. She smiled and told Jack that she had the information and called the rental agent. They had an appointment to look at the apartment on Saturday. Jack was pleased and told Agnes that she thinks of everything.

Jack and Agnes saw the apartment that Saturday and could not believe their eyes. It was a first floor apartment with three bedrooms and a large kitchen. It had a club basement and another bedroom on the basement level. The apartment had two full baths with a new refrigerator and a new stove. Jack and Agnes were very pleased with what they saw. They applied for the apartment and tried not to get their hopes up too high. Agnes told Jack that she felt they would get the apartment. Many people had applied for the apartment including a couple that lived on the third floor of that same building. A week later, Jack and Agnes received a letter stating that they met the eligibility criteria for the apartment. Jack and Agnes were counting their blessings as good things began to happen once more. Jack also informed Agnes that he had received his test scores from the city and was placed on eligibility lists for various civil service jobs. Two weeks later Jack received a letter for an interview with the city.

CHAPTER TEN

...New Job-New Apartment-New Start

Jack was interviewed for a position with the Anti-poverty Agency. The Community Action Agency offered Jack a job as a Neighborhood Development Asst. Counselor. Jack accepted the job and thus started his career with the city of Baltimore. Little did he know that this would be the start of a career that would span the next thiry years of employment with Baltimore city. His starting date was June 9, 1966.

Jack and Agnes settled into their new apartment. The apartment actually had more space than the house they moved from. The apartment was also less exsepensive to maintain. It was conveniently located, close to Agnes's parents and within walking distance to Jack's family. The club basement was very large and modern and served as a facility for many of the family's functions. Jack and Agnes enjoyed entertaining family and friends at their apartment. They never needed a baby sitter because most of the functions were held at this apartment. From Saturday night fish frys to birthday parties or just get togethers. Agnes's sisters and her aunts prepared food for most of the functions. Jack's brothers-in-law and his father in-law became regular visitors. Jack really enjoyed their company. Jack also became closer to his family. He was not as defensive as he had been. His family began to visit him more and more at this apartment. It was like a magnet, everyone was drawn to it. Jack hosted a party for one of his sisters there. It was amazing the number of people that their apartment held. It was that large. It became the official place for New Year's parties.

Things were really going very well for Jack and Agnes. Jack enjoyed his job as a community organizer and was able to enrol in school to take additional courses toward his degree. Jack became closer to his family and began to visit them more often. The time Jack spent with Agnes's family did not go unnoticed by some members of his family. It often became a topic of discussion for some of his family. Agnes being the thoughtful, and considerate person she was would remind Jack to attend more functions that his family had. The pain had eased and Jack became more sensitive to his mother's wishes. He never loved his family any less, but now he was making a conscious effort to please them and spend more time with them. He really missed his brothers and sisters.

Jack was adjusting to his schedule at work and the courses he took for evening school. Jack seemed to have endless energy when it came to balancing his family life, work and school. As busy as Jack was, he always had time for his family. He and Agnes did not go out very much unless they were visiting family members. When they did, they always had Agnes's mom and her sister(Sandy) who were very willing to keep the two girls. Sandy was expecting a child of her own and was always willing to baby sit for Jack and Agnes. Soon, Sandy gave birth to a baby girl. She was a welcomed addition to a loving family. Agnes and her daughters spent a lot of time with Sandy and the new baby.

Both Jack and Agnes came from large families. They were quite aware of the responsibilities and hardships that went along with large families. Large families certainly had a lot of positive sides, but a young married couple with goals and objectives must remain focused on what they wanted to accomplish before being weighed down with the responsibilities of raising a large family.

Jack and Agnes talked about what they needed to do about planning the size of their family. Jack knew that this was a very delicate issue with Agnes which had to be handled just right. Agnes was a devout Catholic that was deeply rooted in her religion. Jack discussed using some form of contraceptives. This seemed to bother Agnes a great deal. She asked Jack if he would agree to talk with the priest at her church. Jack reluctantly agreed to talk to the priest. Agnes arranged for the priest to visit their home to discuss their options.

The Meeting

The priest from Agnes's church was very prompt. Agnes asked Jack to come in and meet the priest. This priest had only been at the parish for one year. Agnes was very quiet during the meeting, but very attentive. Jack had agreed that he would be on his best behavior. Jack informed the priest of the issue facing Agnes and himself. He shared his concern about Agnes's health and that they were interested in using some form of birth control to help manage and plan the size of their family.

The priest did not have to think twice about his answer. He stated very pointedly that this was unacceptable. He was an older man that seemed to be set in his ways. He did not seem willing to deviate from the Catholic dogma at all. The priest was very stern and did not seem interested in the hardship faced by this young couple. Agnes could see that Jack was trying very hard to be respectable and control his responses. He asked the priest what about Agnes' health and the priest did not bend an inch. Jack could see that he was not getting anywhere with this situation. As far as Jack was concerned there was no point in continuing this conversation. With that the meeting was over. Jack had no more questions of the priest. It did not help the situation that the priest was white. This was the sixties and the civil rights movement was in full swing. Jack was known to be somewhat militant at times and very much resented the priest's paternalistic attitude. Because of his wife, whom he loved very much Jack made every effort to be very cooperative.

After the priest left their home, Agnes approached Jack and told him she was very pleased that he handled the situation very responsibly. Jack responded by saying he started to ask the priest to leave but did not. He told Agnes that the decision was their's to make and he was going to do what was necessary to protect her health and reach their goals. Agnes held out her hand and said to Jack" I know." Jack did not want to say anything to upset Agnes. He stated they would find a solution that they both could live with. Agnes smiled and Jack held her in his arms for awhile.

Jack knew that he had to do everything in his power to assist Agnes with this matter. She did not complain a lot when she was not feeling well, but Jack could always tell. He would care for the children more so Agnes could get the rest she needed. There were many times Jack would serve Agnes breakfast in bed. He really enjoyed spoiling her.

New Addition On the Way

Jack noticed one morning before he left for work that Agnes was not feeling well. He asked Agnes what was wrong. She stated that she was feeling nauseous. Jack jokingly said I remember the last time you felt like that you were pregnant. Agnes looked at him without smiling and said. "Well". You're kidding, Jack replied. I wish I was said Agnes. Jack smiled, and said don't be sad sweet heart. Agnes stated she wanted to return to work so she could help out financially, Jack told her in time sweet heart, in time. Jack loved to pamper Agnes and do things for her especially when she was pregnant.

Jack's job as a community organizer often kept him out late. He often had to break up his day and attend neighborhood meetings at night. He always stopped and picked up Chinese food on his way home. Agnes was always waiting for him. The girls were asleep and Agnes and Jack enjoyed talking to each other, listening to jazz and eating their Chinese food. They enjoyed each other's company while discussing their future. Jack enjoyed working for the city because of the flexibility the job allowed. His supervisors also encouraged him to work towards completing his college education.

Jack and Agnes' third child was born in the spring of 1967. The civil rights movement was in full swing and the mood of the country was not very tolerable towards peolpe of color or anyone that was different. Jack enjoyed his work in the neighborhoods because it kept him abreast of the needs and programs that were working and those that were not.

Jack shared with Agnes the experiences of his job and how government agencies interacted with various segments of the community. Jack worked for an agency that would often have to do battle with other agencies in order to obtain services for residents of disadvantaged areas. His job was to assist area residents in obtaining needed services and advocate for those that had problems gaining accsess to the system. His job was supposed to be non-political but he often found himself and his agency in the middle of some very political issues. That was just fine with many of the managers and the executive director of that agency. The agency director was a trained social worker and an administrator that went on to become the first black congressman from Maryland. He never backed down from a good fight and supported his workers when they were right and fought for benefits for those the agency was charged to provide services for. Because of advocacy for the disadvantaged the Agency was constantly at odds with those in the community that were ripping off the poor. Many times it meant being at odds with other government agencies whose goal and mission was to provide services for the community. Jack was one of many young actvists who enjoyed the work they were doing in the community.

Jack had not talked with his friend (James) for some time. He and Agnes ran across James and his wife(Connie) at the super market. Jack asked James how his job at the steel mill was going. James informed Jack that he was ready to look for something else. Jack told James that the Community Action Agency was looking to hire more community activists. He advised James to get his name on the list. Jack told James he would also tell his supervisor about him. James was excited about the posibilities. He thanked Jack and asked him to keep in touch.

Five or six weeks passed when Jack received a call from James informing him that he was on the eligibility list and had received a letter for an interview. He informed Jack that he wanted to use him as a reference. Jack was very happy for his friend. He knew that James had a lot to offer the agency. The possibility of having his best friend working with him again was very exciting.

James was hired by the city and went to work in a neighborhood center in West Baltimore. This location was not far from where Jack worked. They often had lunch together and discussed various aspects of the job. They ran across each other at the monthly meetings at the agency's headquarters. The first six months into the job went very well for James. His supervisor announced at the general meetings how pleased he was to have him on board.

After a year on the job things took a 180 degree turn. James began to lose a lot of time on the job. He called out using many frequencies of sick leave. His supervisor talked with him and he stated he was under his doctor's care. James assured his supervisor that the problem was under control and his attendance would get better. The absenteeism did not get any better. His supervisor called Jack knowing they were good friends. He spoke to Jack off the record informing him of his concerns for his friend. Jack appreciated the information and knew this was a very delicate situation that had to be handled carefully.

Jack contacted James and stated that he missed the lunch time conversations and the company of his friend. James informed Jack that he had been under the weather suffering with a bad case of the flu that he could not shake. He stated that he was under the doctor's care and would return to work soon. Jack asked if he could stop by after work to chat with him. James informed his buddy that he did not need a special invitation or permission to stop by. When Jack arrived, his friend was very happy to see him. James did not look very good, but Jack did not mention anything about his appearance. They talked for a short time and James assured him that his doctor had given him the green light to return to work. Jack noticed that James' wife (Connie) was very quiet the entire time of his visit. Jack talked with Connie briefly, she smiled but did not engage in much conversation. Their little girl had just turned two years old and was saying a few words. She wanted uncle Jack to play with her. Jack held her and played with her awhile. He informed James that he would bring Agnes and the children by for a visit and he left.

Jack was not aware that James had been drinking heavily. He would learn later that his friend's condition was made much worse by his drinking.

Jack did not know at the time that this would be the last time he would see his buddy alive. James was not telling Jack everything. James was suffering from a kidney disorder and a liver disease. Weeks later Jack received a call from James's mother stating that her son was dead. Jack almost dropped the phone. He rushed to James and Connie's apartment as the coroner was removing his body. Connie informed Jack that when she came home from work she found James on the floor with their baby sitting close by. Jack was devastated. He had no idea his friend was that sick. Connie informed

Jack that James forbade her from talking about his condition to anyone. She wanted so much to share this information with Jack on his last visit He especially did not want Jack to know about his illness. Jack wondered if there was something he could have done considering how close he and James were. This was the first time Jack had lost a close friend other than friends lost in the Viet Nam War. It would be a long time before he would get over this death.

CHAPTER ELEVEN

...Crisis in the Nation

The year is 1968 and the civil rights movement is on the fast track with a very capable young minister by the name of Dr. Martin Luther King JR. leading the charge. Dr. King tried to attend every cause he could to lend his support for justice and equality. It was April,1968 and Dr. King was in Memphis, Tenn. to support the garbage workers strike in that city. On April 4, 1968 Dr. King was assasinated. Jack was at work at one of the neighborhood centers when he heard the news. The same feeling came over the community when President Kennedy was shot. It was bad news for the nation but it was a catastrophe for the Black community. In the Black community that grief was soon replaced with anger. They knew they had lost probably the best leader the community ever had. The anger was followed by destruction of the magnitude this nation had never seen.

Many people in Baltimore saw what was happening in other urban areas in the nation. The leaders here felt that Baltimore would not erupt with the civil disobedience and riots like other cities. Then it happened. The eastside, the westside, the city was burning. Frustated citizens had taken to the street. The mayor, and Govenor called for the activation of the National Guard. The city and state police could not handle the magnitude of the problem. Black leaders were approached to help calm the situation.

One agency that the city called on was the Community Action Agency. A meeting was convened and Neighborhood Development Counselors and Asst. Counselors were called upon to help calm the community. It was felt that because of their close working ties with the community they could be effective. This assignment was on a volunteer basis. The group had to be given a special pass by the commander of the National Guard because much of their work had to be done after dark during curfew. Much of their assignment was to escort people to their homes from work and from hospitals.

Jack had never experienced this level of destruction or a community under seige. During the day one could see the state police, and the national guard patrolling the community. On one occasion just outside of Jack's apartment was a truck filled with regular army troops. Jack could not believe that he saw a contingent of troops from the 82nd. airborne outside his door. They were not patrolling but were there in case they were needed. This was a truck load of "brothers" sent there to equalize other brothers. One night Jack got the call to go to University Hospital to escort a young man home that was caught in a cross fire after leaving work. He was not seriously hurt, but could not travel unescorted without fear of being stopped by police or the national guard. Jack traveled with another counselor and could not believe what he saw on his way to the hospital. Jack and his partner had their special passes and a pass for their vehicle to go through the check points. It was like riding through a war zone with check points on every corner. Everyone was being stopped. Each check point was manned by city police from the tactical unit, state police and the national guard. They were all heavily armed. All of this fire power to face for the most part unarmed people that were fed up with a system that had dealt with them in the most unjust ways. This was an experience that Jack would never forget. When he got home he shared this experience with Agnes. He just held her and his youngest child who was almost one year old.

After things had cooled down and returned as close as it could get to being normal. Jack and those members of his agency that had served during this crisis were recognized by the director of the agency and the mayor of the city for playing a crucial role in keeping things calm. Once the violence subsided, came the task of rebuilding the community. Many of the participants in the disturbance were venting their frustration with a system that neglected them for so long. The communities that were destroyed were where the poorest families lived. Grocery stores, liquor stores, pawn shops and small mom and pop stores were hit the hardest. This left a void in the community and the residents suffered. The destruction of these establishments that catered primarily to the poor and black neighborhoods would be felt for some time.

Many of the residents did a lot of their shopping and business at the neighborhood stores and did not have the means to travel to other areas to shop. Never mind that many of these stores were ripping them off, but without them it left the affected communities hard pressed to obtain their basic needs. Soup lines were set up and many of the social agencies including the Community Action Agency where Jack was employed was suddenly in the business of food distribution.

This was not only a rough period for the black communities affected by the civil disobedience, but also for the country as a whole. It showed the world and some American citizens who were oblivious to the plight of Black Americans a side of the country that had been hidden from view for too long. The conditions in the country would not change over night. It took the death of a prominent leader like Dr. Martin Luther King Jr. (whose philosophy of non-violence in the struggle for justice and equality earned him the Nobel Peace prize) to bring these conditions out in the open. This shamed the nation into taking some corrective action in the area of social justice. As the undisputed leader of the free world, the United States did not have any problems pointing the finger at nations they suspected of human rights violations. Many countries accused the Americans of being hypocrits.

Return To Normalcy

For the next few years, Jack and Agnes focused on the development of their young family. They grew closer as a family. Jack took advantage of every oportunity to continue his education. His employment with the city gave him the flexibility to take courses related to his job. Although it would take him longer to complete his college education, this did not change his focus. He managed to balance work, school and still spend quality time with his family. Jack received one promotion with the city agency where he worked, but knew he would have to have his degree to continue to move up the ladder. He has four years of service with Baltimore City and is moving closer to obtaining his degree.

Even with his very busy schedule, Jack still remained tuned in to his family's needs. He often talked to Agnes about their growing family and the best way to raise them. Jack noticed that Agnes seemed to have less and less energy. He often took the children out in order to give her some rest and quiet time. Jack encouraged Agnes to seek medical attention. Agnes was found to be anemic. She had been suffering with the condition of anemia for some time. She was given medication and after a couple of weeks her condition improved dramatically.

Agnes and Jack enjoyed the nice apartment they had, but realized they wanted a better environment for their children. The idea of home ownership was once again a topic for discussion. The girls were attending the Catholic primary school where Agnes received her elementary education. The couple agreed they needed to plan for this move along with other objectives they had.

Agnes Returns To Work

Agnes realized that in order for her and Jack to make some of their dreams a reality, there had to be some additional income coming into the house. She knew Jack would try to do everything by himself, but did not want him to become overburdened. Agnes knew Jack was very protective of her and would consider her health. She was now doing much better and with all the help he was giving her, she felt strong enough to go to work. The problem as she saw it was to convince Jack that she was well enough to go to work.

Agnes had a gift that allowed her to do very well with young children. She used to earn extra income babysitting. She had the patience and knowledge necessary to provide good care for her clients. Her customers told her she was a natural teacher. She convinced Jack she would try to find something in the area of child development. Jack felt relieved to know that she was not considering returning to sewing.

Agnes had very good public relation skills, which landed her a job at the telephone company. The job was as a long distance operator. It was not a bad job, but the working conditions were not very good for her and her young family. She got off from work very late and Jack was always worried when he was not able to pick her up. This job did not last very long and Jack was not upset when Agnes told him she would resign because she was not able to get an earlier shift. She managed to stay there almost one year.

Agnes used to volunteer at one of the public schools in the neighborhood, and she got a very pleasant surprise one day. The principal of that school watched how well she worked with the children and encouraged her to apply for a position as a teacher's assistant. She completed the application and passed the exam with flying colors. She shared this information with Jack. She tried not to get to excited, but Jack told her that this was her calling. He watched how patient and loving she was with children and knew she would do well at this job. She kept telling Jack that she did not have the job yet, but Jack knew with the principal's recommendation it was only a matter of time.

Within a couple of weeks of notification of being on the employment list, Agnes received a call from the principal's secretary to come in for an interview. Agnes was elated. She could not wait to tell Jack the good news. Very soon after the interview, Agnes was hired by the Department of Education.

A few months into the job as a teacher's assistant, Jack could see the change in Agnes. She talked about her job with so much enthusiasm. She gave 100 per cent of herself while she was at work. Jack could see that this was very rewarding for Agnes and he supported her in her new found interest. She included Jack in many of the projects she was involved in and often volunteered his services.

Jack and Agnes's youngest child was a toddler and too young for any of the pre-school programs. They would need a baby sitter for their son. The girls were enrolled in pre-school and kindergarten programs. The search for a baby sitter did not take very long. Agnes asked Carolyn(Jack's sister) if she would baby sit for her. Carolyn was not working and was living with Jack's mother. She had a number of school age children and one the same age as Jack Jr. This arrangement worked well because it gave Jack's mother a chance to spend more time with Jack's child.

Jack was very pleased with this arrangement and he knew that Agnes had other family members that she could get to baby sit for her but she wanted to give her children every opportunity to get to know both sides of their family. She also knew that Jack was still very protective when it came to his immediate family because of the ordeal they went through. She did not want her children to suffer because of this. Jack was pleased, but Agnes knew she would have to be the one to take the initiative when it came to these matters. Jack knew he was truly blessed to have such a thoughtful person in his life.

Agnes got Jack Jr. ready each morning. She prepared a little lunch and snacks for him. She put his lunch along with a change of clothes in a small suit case with his name on it. Jack dropped him off each morning and picked him up after work. He cried the first two days, then adjusted quite well. Some days Agnes stopped by with the girls after school and Jack picked up his family after work. Jack's mother smiled and told Jack and Agnes what a wonderful family they had. She was very pleased to see how things were turning out for them. She looked at Jack and smiled and without saying it knew how she misjudged Agnes.

CHAPTER TWELVE

...Changes Are In The Wind

Jack and Agnes were enjoying their family and their jobs allowed them to meet their needs. They managed to save a little money on a regular basis. Agnes had been working for eighteen months and was very pleased with her assignment. Jack managed to continue taking evening courses at college.

With a very busy schedule, they still managed to entertain their friends and family. Their apartment still was the preferred site for most gatherings. As a matter of fact, it soon became the home of one of Agnes's brothers. He had recently gone through a divorce. Jack had a good relationship with all of Agnes's brothers but was especially close to Jerry. When Agnes asked Jack if Jerry could stay with them, it was not a problem at all. Jerry rented a room and had the use of the entire basement. He was very independent and provided for all of his needs.

This arrangement worked out well for a couple of years. Jack's family was getting older and he and Agnes were thinking once again about home ownership. The nest egg they had put away was steadily growing. Their young son was now able to attend the same school where Agnes was employed. They informed Jerry(Agnes's brother) that they would be looking to buy a house soon. He expressed an interest in keeping the apartment once they moved. Jerry was given all the contact information for the management company.

Jack and Agnes looked at a number of houses in their price range but was not sold on any of them. After looking for two or three weeks, the real estate agent called them and said he found the perfect house for them. He took them to a house in the Northwood section of the city. It was a three bedroom house with a paneled club room in the basement. It had hard wood floors throughout. It was a brick house, end of group with a masonry fireplace, a beautiful lawn and flower bed with azaleas all around. It had a fenced yard and a brick garage. Jack and Agnes took one look at the house and knew it was the one for them. It needed a little work but had so much potential. The great thing about this house was the price; It was very affordable. The owner of the house was a widow and wanted it to go to a nice young couple. She felt that Jack and Agnes were the right couple and was willing to help them get the house. Jack and Agnes signed the contract and left a check for the down payment.

Their offer was accepted by the owner. They now had to wait for financing to be approved. There were a couple of issues that needed to be addressed on the credit report. The agent was not overly concerned about this problem. He had Jack write a letter explaining the reason for slow pay on one of his accounts. There were no bills or accounts that were not paid in full. A few weeks later the agent called with the news they were hoping to here. They were approved for financing. The loan was guaranteed by the FHA(Federal Housing Administration). When it was inspected there were some improvements that needed to be made. Jack agreed to make some of the needed repairs when the owner agreed to lower the price. Some of the improvements were as simple as painting a couple of rooms.

The Move To A New Home

After the closing, Jack and Agnes were free to move into their new home. Before they moved in, Jack and Agnes went by the house to see what changes they wanted to make. Agnes had a flair for decorating and decided to change the color scheme a little. Her father was an experienced painter and offered his service. Jack's brother, his brother-in-law, and his father-in-law helped them prepare for the move. When they were ready to move in, Jack's brother rented and drove the truck to help them move. They had so much help from family members they did not need to hire any outside contractors. Everyone was willing to help Jack and Agnes. They were kind hearted and did anything to help others. Everyone could see that they struggled to make a good life with very meager means. They kept a positive attitude while trying to reach their goals.

Jack gets Promoted

Jack and Agnes barely settled into their new home before Jack received notification from the Baltimore City Health Department to come for an interview as a public health representative in the Bureau of Disease Control. Jack believed in completing applications and applying for positions that were open with the city. As a result of taking the tests and being placed high on the eligibility lists, Jack was called by various city agencies. The interview for the job went very well. Jack informed Agnes that he felt he would get the job with the health department. Agnes smiled and told Jack she was very happy he felt that way but don't get overjoyed before it was official. Jack agreed and tried to resume his usual routine.

Two weeks went by, then Jack received a letter from the Baltimore City Health Dept. personnel office telling him he had the job. It had his starting date and where he should report. His starting salary was increased and his time of service with the city would continue uninterrupted. To celebrate, Jack invited some family and friends over and had a cook out. He bought some crabs and fired up the grill. He and Agnes generally celebrated special occasions by having close friends and relatives over.

Jack reported to his new job as scheduled. After a brief orientation at the main office, he was informed about the district where he would be assigned. His immediate supervisor was on vacation for two weeks. Jack started his training immediately. He familiarized himself with the chest clinic personnel and procedures.

When his immediate supervisor returned to work, he stopped by to see Jack at his assignment at the Eastern Health District. His name was Jerome McCoy. He talked with Jack about his job function and responsibilities. As a public health representative, he would supervise four or five health aides in the chest clinic. They were responsible for follow up on patients that were diagnosed with tuberculosis. These were patients that were non-compliant in keeping their clinic visits and continuing their medications. Jack learned very quickly to work with the nursing staff and scheduled home visits for the health aides under his supervision. His staff was also responsible for contact investigation on newly diagnosed cases.

Once a month the supervisory staff met downtown at the main office to discuss statistics and measure achievements of staff. At one particular meeting, Jerome McCoy kept looking at Jack and asked if he had any brothers. He mentioned to Jack that there was a guy by the same last name that went to high school with him. His name was Moses. He went by the nickname of "Bull". Jack said that's my brother. He's next to the oldest. Jerome said I knew you had that familiar look. There was an instant bond between Jack and Jerome. They became close friends.

Jerome often told Jack about his experience of talking with his oldest brother(Teddy) when he came home from Korea as a prisoner of war. He stated that he never experienced a gathering like the one they had for him. The entire community was involved including politicians. He told Jack that Moses informed everyone in their class of his brother's experiences in the war. Jerome told Jack that his brother(Teddy)was a hero to all of them.

Jerome and Jack met each other's family and went on picnics together. Jerome had three boys and Jack had two girls and a boy. They visited each other's homes and socialized together. Jerome informed Jack that he was one of the most responsible and productive workers he ever supervised.

Jack worked for the Bureau of Disease Control for the next four years. One thing he accomplished while working for this bureau was getting his degree from Morgan State University. He was able to get his final course work done by adjusting his work schedule. His final two courses were only offered during the day and Jack got permission to use his lunch hour to achieve this.

Jack gets his college degree

Jack informed Agnes that he had completed his course work toawrds his degree. He had to wait for the next semester to graduate because the graduations were only in May. That really did not bother Jack. The most important thing was that he had accomplished one of the goals he set for himself. Agnes played a very significant part in this accomplishment as did Jack's mother. They both supported Jack in the things he wanted to do, but went about it in different ways.

This was extremely important to Jack, because he and Agnes struggled to keep a balance in their immediate family while moving forward under sometimes difficult conditions. It took Jack longer to get his last year of college than it did to complete his first three years.

He was not at all interested in the pomp and circumstance but obtaining a degree that he knew would result in more promotions and job opportunities. He paid the usual class fees and graduating expenses. The day of his graduation he sat in the audience as his name was called. After the exercises, he went to his department to pick up his degree. He celebrated with Agnes and a few close friends by having a cookout in his back yard. His children, still very young were very happy for their daddy. Later that night before Agnes and Jack went to bed they talked. He thanked Agnes for being there for him and acknowledged to her that he was not sure he could have done it without her. Agnes looked at Jack and saw the tears rolling down his face. She said, "Jack, I love you". She embraced Jack and they both cried and held each other. Jack was thinking about all the obstacles they had to overcome and the many sacrifices they both made. He shared with Agnes that there wasn't anything that he could not accomplish with her by his side. Jack told Agnes she was truly the glue that held their family together. They talked a little while longer and went to sleep in each others arms.

Agnes becomes Ill

A month after the graduation Agnes was not feeling very well. Jack noticed that she did not have very much energy and was not very patient with the children. He did extra things around the house and got the children involved in exercises to keep them busy. Jack took them shopping with him and to amusement parks. Jack cooked and did everything he could to let Agnes get some rest.

This time, Agnes didn't get any better even with all the rest. She woke up one morning complaining of pains in her stomach and pelvic area. Agnes was not one to complain unless she was in severe pain. Jack knew that something was wrong. Agnes made an appointment to see her doctor. Upon examination, the doctor sent her to a specialist. She went through a series of tests. The doctor found that she had a number of tumors in her pelvic area. This frightened her very much. After getting over the initial shock, she told Jack what was found. Jack and Agnes met with the gynecologist for further explanation. He informed them that the extent of the surgery would be determined by what was found when they operated. He also explained that Agnes may need a total hysterectomy.

The doctor shared with them that if this is the case, Agnes would not be able to have anymore children. Jack and Agnes decided to do whatever was necessary to improve Agnes's health. They decided to go ahead with the surgery.

Agnes received her date for the scheduled surgery. She and Jack prepared the family for her surgery. Jack took Agnes to the hospital early on the day of her surgery. The surgery lasted for several hours. Agnes went to the recovery room after the long surgery. The doctors told Jack that they removed three tumors from Agnes. One was the size of a grapefruit. The good news was they were benign. The bad news was that they had to perform a total hysterectomy. Agnes was still in the recovery room and very groggy.

When she was taken to a room Jack spent the rest of the day with her. She asked about the children. Jack informed her that thay were doing fine. They were at her mothers' house being cared for by Sandy and Miss Helen. Agnes spent several more days in the hospital and at least six to eight weeks recuperating at home. This would give Jack a chance to spoil her even more.

When Agnes came home, Jack insisted that she follow the doctors orders exactly. Her sister(Sandy) was a big help with the children. At times, Sandy became impatient with Jack Jr. and told Jack he needed to do something with him. Jack talked with him and sometimes dropped him pass his mother's house. After a few weeks, Sandy saw how Jack was doing every thing for Agnes and told her she was lazy and spoiled. Jack just laughed and said that's my baby. I don't care if I have to do everthing for her. He told Agnes to take all the time she needed to get better. Sandy said, "How disgusting".

Eventually, Agnes's health improved. She was now feeling well enough to return to work at the school system. Having spent her entire summer convalescing she was eager to get back to work. Jack always felt very good when he saw Agnes with a smile on her face.

She told Jack that she really felt quite well.

Agnes returns to work

The day Agnes returned to work she was wearing a navy blue business suit. Jack complimented her on the way she looked. She stated she dressed like this because the students would not return until a week later. This past summer was quite an experience for Jack and his family. Jack completed all the shopping with the help of the oldest two girls. They were a big help. They also helped to care for Jack Jr. Although he felt he did not need anyone to look after him.

A few weeks into the school routine, Jack could see that Agnes was really into her work. Jack saw how much pleasure this job gave her. She often shared the experiences she had with her students with Jack. Jack encouraged Agnes to go back to school to get a degree in early childhood education. She told Jack that was what she really wanted to do. She wanted to teach school at the elementary level. She was interested in the education and development of young children. She felt that it was so important to get them off to a good start. She cared about the children and was very involved in their learning process.

Jack encouraged Agnes to enrol in college taking courses in the evening and during the summer sessions. He gave her all the support she needed in helping her to complete this goal.

Meanwhile Jack continued to place his name on eligibility lists for jobs with the city. He enjoyed his work with the Health Department's Bureau of Disease Control, but knew there were no promotions in the foreseeable future. Jack always looked at the civil service job announcements and submitted applications for the positions he was interested in.

Job Promotion for Jack

Jack received notification from the civil service commission that his name was placed on the eligibility list for another bureau in the health department His name was also placed on lists with other city agencies. Jack received a letter from the Bureau of Special Home Services to come in to interview for the position of Home Services aide Supervisor II. Jack interviewed for that position and felt confident that he would get the job. Jack shared with Agnes that if he was offered the job he would accept it. This would continue his service with the health department. Jack already had ten years of service with the city of Baltimore. A few weeks passed, then Jack received the news he was hoping to hear. Jack was offered the job with the Bureau of Special Home Services.

Once again, life was going well for Jack and Agnes. Their children were well and Agnes was doing well. Jack was very thankful that he and his family were receiving these blessings.

CHAPTER THIRTEEN

Tragedy strikes again

While things were going well for Jack and Agnes, Their parents were not as fortunate.

Agnes's mother had been suffering with diabetes and heart trouble for years. Her health was slowly deteriorating. Her sight was failing her, and her mobility was limited. She was constantly there for all of her children and grandchildren. The demands on her time grew with her advancing age.

Jack was having a difficult time dealing with the failing health of his father. His father lived alone in an apartment complex not far from him. Jack with the help of one of his older brothers(Moses) checked on their father regularly. Jack was concerned about his father's drinking and forgetfulness. His father was very lonely and had people visit his apartment that did not have his best interest at heart. These were individuals Jack did not trust. Occasionally, his father visited him and shared an evening with his family. He always liked to have a drink and that concerned Jack. Jack reluctantly had a drink with his father. When it came time for him to leave, Jack walked him to his car to make sure he was alright. He stated he was quite capable of driving himself home. Thirty minutes later Jack received a call from his father stating he could not find his way home. Jack asked where he was and told him to stay there until he arrived. Once Jack got there, he made sure his father was okay then told him to follow him to his apartment. Since that incident, Jack decided to visit his father at his apartment so he would not have to drive. Jack felt much better about this arrangement. He picked his father up on occasions so he could share an evening with Jack's family.

On one of Jack's visits, he had a problem waking his father up. He took a long time answering his door. When he did, Jack rushed to the kitchen to turn off a pot of food that was burning. This was not the first time his father went to sleep with food on the stove. Another problem Jack found out about was his father forgetting to mail his rent to the management company. Jack had to intercede a couple of times so his father would not be evicted. Jack's older brother tried to help, and for awhile he handled their father's finances. This would not continue because their father wanted to be in control and felt he could handle the situation.

Eventually, things got to the point where the management company would not accept rent and wanted Jack's father to move. Jack spoke with the manager of the complex and the manager stated that his father was putting everyone in the complex at risk. The fire department was called on the latest occasion and the manager would not accept any more rent. His father asked Jack to store some of his furniture in his garage. He told Jack he would rent a room with one of his old friends.

This arrangement worked for awhile, but Jack's father was used to having his own place. He called Jack a couple of times and tried to sound upbeat, but Jack knew he was going through some difficult times. His father was very proud and stubborn and it was difficult to assist him. He would stop by the liquor store on payday and cash his check. He purchased liquor and sat in his car to drink it. The store had a large parking lot on its premises. The owner of the store knew him very well and would let him sit there for awhile. This happened on a number of occasions and the owner became concerned with his safety. He knew the gentleman that Jack's father was staying with and called to let him know his concerns. Mr. Battle(friend of Jack's father) called to let Moses and Jack know what was going on. The brothers took turns looking after their father. Moses's wife cooked for him and did his laundry. After awhile, Moses backed off and Jack took over. This was very difficult for the brothers because so much emotion was involved in this situation. They could help the father as long as they did things his way. He was not the kind of person that accepted advice from his sons. One would have to be very diplomatic to get him to accept constructive criticism. Jack was better at this than Moses. There were a few times when he actually made some progress. He and his father even talked about trying to find a small apartment where Jack and Moses could check on him on a regular basis. His father soon fell back in his same pattern and then Moses took over for awhile. Jack's father started his drinking again and went to sleep in his car behind the liquor store. Moses went over to see about him this time and found him in a bad way. His father was very sick and could not offer much resistance. Moses took him to the hospital.

Meanwhile, Jack and Agnes were with her mother who was was very ill. These were some trying times for Jack and Agnes. Miss Helen was having difficulty keeping her blood glucose levels in the normal range. Agnes sat and talked with her mother while Jack spent time with his father-in-law. When Jack got home later that night, he received a call from Moses telling him that their father had pneumonia and developed a blood clot. The next day, Jack picked up his mother and went to the hospital. His father was in a good mood and talked about getting out of the hospital. Although Jack's parents were separated, they were very happy to see each other. Jack's mother always told Jack to check on his father. Although they were separated, she was still very much concerned about him.

Jack and Agnes tried very hard to shelter their children from the distress they were experiencing. Their oldest daughter was very perceptive and knew her parents were going through difficult times. Jack seemed to be handling the situation a lot better than Agnes. Agnes was the baby in her family and extremely close to her mother. She could not hide her emotions from her children.

A couple of days went by without any changes. After Jack and Agnes had dinner with the children they talked about their parents' situation. The children completed their homework and were getting ready for bed. About nine pm. that night the telephone rang. It was Agnes's father on the line. He told Jack he was glad he answered the phone. He had bad news. Agnes's mother died of a heart attack and he did not want to tell Agnes over the phone. Jack said he would take care of it. It took Jack a couple of minutes to compose himself before he delivered the bad news. He went to Agnes and put his arms around her and told her what had happened. All Agnes could say was "Oh mama! Oh mama"!

They dressed all the children, loaded them in the car and went to her mother's house. When Jack and Agnes arrived, they were met by other sibblings and relatives.

The next couple of days were spent with Agnes's father and other relatives of hers. It was exactly two days after Miss Helen's death while Jack and Agnes were making funeral arrangements with her brothers and sisters that Jack received a phone call. It was his brother, Moses calling from the hospital. He informed Jack that his father had just died at the hospital. The blood clot had moved to his lungs and had caused an embolism. Jack was stunned. He could not believe what was happening. The look on his face said it all. Agnes knew it was more bad news. He told Agnes what happened. They both cried and just held each other. Jack asked Agnes if she would be alright. She told Jack to go to the hospital to be with his family. She was okay because she was surrounded by her family. Jack left quickly while Agnes explained to her family what occurred.

The events of the past week was truly a test of the young couple's faith. They had to rely very deeply on their faith and their belief that God would not put any more on them than they could bear. These events left both of them emotionally drained. They took some time off from work just to be with each other and appreciate each other. This experience brought them closer to each other and more in love. Their committment to each other was now stronger than ever. They realized that they had each other to help overcome any obstacle or event that was placed in their path.

Well deserved Vacation

A few months after the deaths in their family, Jack thought seriously about a vacation for Agnes and himself. They always planned outings that were shared with the children and other family members. These were generally day trips or picnics.

Jack's father was a long term employee of a company that dealt with a large steel company. He had a share account with that company that had the names of all ten of his children as beneficiaries. In addition to the share account, he listed Moses and Jack as beneficiaries of an insurance policy that the company kept in force for him. This gave Jack a little extra income that he did not have to pay bills with.

When Jack asked Agnes about taking a vacation she always said they could not afford it. Jack really wanted to do something nice for Agnes. They never had a honeymoon or any vacation to speak of. Jack's oldest sister(Mildred) and her husband(Alfred) were planning a trip to the Bahamas and Jack felt this would be a perfect vacation for Agnes and himself. He often confided in Mildred and at times asked her advice on certain issues. As for Alfred, he was more than a brother-in-law, Jack considered him to be one of his closest friends. As far as Jack was concerned, it was settled. He told Agnes that he was planning a trip for them to the Bahamas. She said," The Bahamas." Yes, the Bahamas said Jack. Agnes told Jack they could not afford to go on that trip. I know you want to do something nice for us but,...Jack interrupted. No buts...we are going. He looked at Agnes and said to her, "Baby, we can't afford not to go." I love you and would like to do this for you. Tomorrow is not promised and we both deserve this trip. Agnes smiled at Jack and said why not. She was so happy. It was so delightful for Jack to see that wonderful smile come back on Agnes's face.

This trip turned out to be one of the best remedies for emotional fatigue and depression. Jack and Agnes fell in love with the wonderful beaches and the night life in the Bahamas. This was their first trip to Nassau, Bahamas and Paradise Island. Mildred and Alfred had made the trip a few times before. They met a wonderful family on the Island that they corresponded with regularly. They introduced Jack and Agnes to this lovely lady that was affectionately called

"Sistah." She was one of the friendliest persons Jack and Agnes ever met. She owned and operated a business in the world famous straw market. She invited the entire group to her home for a wonderful dinner. Jack and Agnes also got an opportunity to visit her church.

Agnes and Jack shopped for gifts for the children and other relatives. This was the most enjoyable seven days that Jack and Agnes had ever spent on any trip. Agnes thanked Jack over and over for encouraging her to take the trip. Jack turned to Agnes and said, "Thank you for being the person you are." They agreed that they should take a trip like this one at least once a year. It was so good for the two of them to have that time together. They continued to plan family trips that included their children and other family members, but they also realized the benefit of a trip for just the two of them.

CHAPTER FOURTEEN

...Facing Reality and Renewing Trust

After a very refreshing vacation, Jack and Agnes returned to continue with their lives. The next five or six months would be very difficult for this couple. Jack grew closer to his father in his later years. Although, the additional responsibility of looking out for his father left him emotionally drained, Jack missed him very much. He now realized that he had developed a bond with his father that was not there while he was growing up. It is true that he worried a lot about his father, but he got an opportunity to fill a void and enjoyed his father's company. His father was a great talker and always had some very interesting stories that he shared with him.

Agnes took her mother's death very hard. Because she was the baby in her family, she spent a lot of time in her mother's company. She was at home as a teenager when her mother's sickness began and was there to comfort her. When Jack was courting Agnes, he always saw her sitting on the steps with her mother. If her mother was not on the steps, she was looking out the window. This relationship continued after Jack and Agnes got married. Not a week went by that Agnes did not visit her mother. She often had Jack pick her and the children up from Miss Helen's house. Jack, Agnes and the children spent nearly every weekend visiting Agnes's parents.

Agnes missed her mother very much. She sat quietly at times just staring at her mother's picture. Jack knew she missed her a lot. He did everything he could to comfort her. Her biggest comfort was to have Jack put his arms around her and just hold her. After holding her for awhile, she finally responded. Jack told her that her mother was alright. She is no longer in pain. She is being cared for by her father in heaven. Agnes told Jack how blessed she was to have him in her life. He told Agnes that he thanked God for sending him an angel like herself.

Agnes continued to go to the same church that she and her mother went to on a regular basis. Sometimes Jack went with her and the children. Other times he dropped them off and went to his church. The two older children went to the parochial school for part of their elementary education. When Jack and Agnes moved to their new home the girls were transferred to the neighborhood public school. The couple's son was transferred from the public school where Agnes worked to a Catholic school in the neighborhood. Jack and Agnes felt he would benefit from the special attention in the smaller school. After a year, Agnes and the children joined St. Mathew's Catholic churh in the neighborhood and became active in the church. Periodically, she returned to St. Pius V, to be close to her roots.

Agnes kept herself busy by being involved in her childrens' lives. Her biological children as well as her children in the classroom. She often stayed at school to assist the children well beyond her scheduled work time. She was teacher, social worker, counselor or whatever the situation called for. Her first priority was to make a difference in the lives of the little ones that she came in touch with. She received a lot of assistance from Jack. Their own children were involved in activities around their schools and the recreation center in their neighborhood. Jack would pick up the children from the rec center after he left work. They shared the responsibility of cooking and preparing meals; however, Jack did most of the cooking. Jack enjoyed cooking and the family seemed to enjoy the dinner better when he cooked. Agnes used to kid with Jack concerning her cooking. She told Jack the food tasted so much better when he prepared it.

There were times when Jack had to wake Agnes up to eat dinner. She was generally very tired when she came in from school. She would lay down to rest for awhile and soon fell into a deep sleep. Jack, always concerned about Agnes's health felt she might be pushing herself too much. He convinced her not to take any summer courses this year. He told her that this summer would be spent traveling with her and the children.

A Summer Of Fun

School was now out and Jack planned a summer of fun for his family. He and Agnes were around her family much of the time. Jack shared with her that he would like to take them on a trip with some of his family. Jack and Agnes enjoyed traveling with his oldest sister and her husband. Alfred and Mildred generally took their two youngest children with them on short trips. This worked out well because they were around the same age as Jack's children. This also gave Jack an opportunity to test his new car on the road. It was a brand new Chrysler Cordoba fully loaded. This was the second new car that Jack and Agnes ever owned. It was a full size luxury car unlike the small Datsun Jack previously owned.

The first trip of the summer was a visit to Virginia Beach and Petersburg Va. Alfred(Jack's brother-in-law) had a friend in the Air Force that was stationed at Fort Lee. They spent the weekend between Virginia Beach and Petersburg. This was a fun trip for everyone. When Jack and Agnes returned home, she told Jack the trip was so invigorating.

After resting for a couple of days they were off to visit Virginia again. This time, more of Jack's family went on the trip including Jack's mother. This pleased Agnes very much to see Jack really enjoying his family. They visited Jack's great uncle who lived in Norfolk, Va. This was Jack's maternal grandfather's brother.

Jack promised his children they would go to King's Dominion some day. What they did not know was, Jack made reservations to stay over night at a hotel outside King's Dominion. The children got a chance to spend the day with their cousins and their grandmother. The entire family enjoyed King's Dominion, and one could see that Jack's mother really enjoyed being with Agnes, Jack and the children.

After returning to Baltimore, Jack and Agnes prepared for the last leg of the vacation. They were going to visit another one of Jack's great uncles and his wife. Agnes looked and felt great. Jack knew the trips were working wonders for her. The trips also brought Jack and his mother closer together. She asked Jack and Agnes if she could ride with them on the trip to Connecticut. They were very happy that she decided to ride with them. The trip meant a lot to Jack's mother. She got a chance to visit with her father's oldest living brother and her favorite aunt.

Jack's family was very excited about the wonderful vacation and the fun they had. The children talked about the trips for the rest of the summer. Agnes told Jack that he always knew what to do to lift her spirits. She often said they could not afford to take a vacation. Jack told her that she and the children deserved to take some time off from their hectic schedule. Jack knew the entire family had been through quite an ordeal. He was so happy that everyone had a good time and there were no problems.

He and Agnes grew more and more in love with each year that passed. Because of the love they had for one another, they were able to face whatever problems life had in store for them.

A Message from Mom

A week after the vacation, Jack's mother called him and told him she would like to talk to him. Jack informed her that he would stop by the house after work. When Jack arrived, she asked him to have a seat. She told Jack that she really enjoyed the vacation. She informed Jack that he was very good about taking her to visit her relatives on long drives like Philadelphia or Scranton, Pa. This last trip meant a lot to her because she really got a chance to see how Jack interacted with his family. She knew Jack was generally alone when he visited her. She asked him to bring his family by to visit more often.

Deep within her heart she knew why Jack did not bring his family by that often. Jack never said why because it was a very delicate situation. He always made excuses, but his mother knew the real reason. She told Jack that he had a loving family, and she was very proud of the job that he and Agnes were doing with the children. She also told Jack that she was wrong about Agnes. Jack could see that it was bothering her and it was very awkward for her. Without actually saying the words, he knew this was her way of saying she was sorry. This lifted a great burden off their shoulders. With that said, she told Jack she baked him his favorite sweet potato bread.

When Jack reached his home, he was quiet and thought about what his mother said. He realized that with all the grandchildren she had, she still missed his children not being around that often. Jack felt he was protecting his family by isolating them. He now knew that this was not necessary. He was so deeply hurt by the events that preceded his marriage that he adopted a defensive and protective attitude when it came to his immediate family.

After meditating for awhile, he talked to Agnes about his visit. She was so in tune with her husband that she knew pretty much what the visit was all about. Jack shared with her the things he and his mother talked about. Agnes was much better at handling the situation than Jack was. She had come to grips with what happened and moved beyond that. Agnes tried many times to get Jack to take the children to visit his mother. She often told Jack that his mother reacted to a situation she felt was not in the best interest of her son. She did not realize that her son had moved beyond the point where he needed her protection. She also told Jack that she had long forgiven his mother for her past actions. Jack looked at Agnes and told her that she was simply amazing. She was truly an angel. Agnes looked at Jack and said," When are we going to eat that sweet potato bread?"

CHAPTER FIFTEEN

...Getting over another hurdle

A few years passed and lo and behold just like clockwork another setback found its way to Jack and Agnes doorstep. This time it was not any family members. Jack, Agnes and the rest of their family were fine.

Jack drove his car to work at the health department every day. He parked at ten hour meters or an inexpensive parking lot off the street. It was in December about a week or a few days before Christmas that Jack's office party for the holidays was given. This was a tradition in the health department and other city agencies to have the party. Jack worked for a bureau in the health department that had a reputation of giving the best Christmas parties in the agency. The staff brought in food they prepared at home as well as some catered menus. For the most part, the party was alcohol free, but it was an unwritten rule to allow a co-worker to make her whiskey sours. Everyone agreed that she made the best whiskey sours they ever tasted. The health commissioner always stopped by to sample the food and drinks. He would smile and say it certainly met the taste test.

The day of the party Jack decided to park his car in the indoor garage because it was closer to the office and Jack always had plenty of gifts to carry. He also knew that the party would go on after work hours. The party was very successful and Jack left with all his gifts to carry to the car. The garage was only a half block away. When Jack reached the garage, he gave the attendant his stub and waited for him to retrieve his car. The attendant was taking a long time to return Jack's car. He noticed other customers getting their cars that came in after he did. Jack called the manager and asked why was it taking so long to return his car. The manager called for the attendant over the speaker. The attendant responded to the manager's call, but there was no car. Jack was begining to get a little nervous. The attendant searched again and informed Jack and the manager that the car was not there. It had been stolen from the garage. Jack could not believe what he heard. How ironic he exclamed; I've parked the car on the street three years and nothing ever happened to it. The first time I use the indoor garage it gets stolen. This is unbelievable.

Jack filed a police report and contacted his insurance company. He was hoping that his car would be found soon without any damage. This was not to be. Days turned to weeks, weeks to a month and still no car. Jack's insurance company was ready to settle the claim with Jack. They sought to be reimbursed by the insurance company for the garage.

Jack was not very thrilled to settle because he was not ready to accept the fact that his car would not be returned to him. The car was paid for and Jack was not ready to take on a new car payment. Jack was paid for the loss of his car, which was determined by the blue book value. This did not seem fair to Jack because he kept his car in very good condition. He knew he would not be able to get the same car for the settlement that the insurance company offered him.

A Time To Move On

Jack had to accept his loss and move on. He needed transportation for himself and his family. He looked at many cars but was not satisfied with any of them. Most of the cars he could afford were too small for his growing family. He began thinking about a van, and asked Agnes what she thought about the family car being a van. Agnes was not thrilled with the idea, but agreed to look at some vans with Jack.

Jack and Agnes looked at some vans but the new ones were too much for their budget. Jack and Agnes decided to look at some used vans. They finally found one they liked. It was a twelve passenger late model Beauville Chevy Van. This was certainly large enough for his growing family of teenagers and a few cousins. Jack purchased the van and he and Agnes showed it off to their family.

A short time after the purchase of the van, Jack received a notice for ten or more overdue parking citations for his stolen car. Jack was so upset he could not believe it. This amounted to hundreds of dollars. Jack contacted the proper authorities who quickly disposed of the matter without Jack having to pay a penny. Jack also noticed that his car had been parked at a parking meter less than a mile from where he lived. He could not understand why after placing two or three tickets on the car it was not checked out to see if it was stolen. This was a perfect example of how city agencies did not coordinate their efforts in the best interest of their citizens.

Jack and Agnes decided not to cry over spilt milk, and made every effort to enjoy their van. Their van became the vehichle of choice when they went on trips or vacations with the family. The van provided plenty of room for their immediate family and others who needed a ride. It also proved to be less expensive for Jack and other relatives to car pool when travelling long distances. This van was very comfortable.

Earning Extra Income

The van turned out to be worth its weight. Not only was it a convenient way for family members to travel, but Jack and Agnes found a way to bring in additional income. Extra money was always needed when it came to three teenage children and a growing list of demands.

It all started one weekend when Jack and Agnes used all of their disposable income to take care of family expenses. Jack got the bright idea to look in his garage to see what was there. He saw many items that the family discarded or would not use any longer. He decided to take two seats out of the van and load the van with these items. He also placed two folding tables in the van and asked Agnes to come with him to the flea market. They had just enough money to get a five dollars worth of gas and ten dollars to set up at the flea market. Something very remarkable happened on that Sunday. After five or six hours at the flea market, Jack and Agnes sold everything on their table. They generated close to two hundred dollars for their efforts. They stopped at a hamburger and sub shop they used to visit when they were teenagers. They bought two large subs and milk shakes. Jack and Agnes split their proceeds, enjoyed their subs and laughed all the way home. They still could not believe the day they had at the flea market.

Agnes always had a flair for designing and fashions. Jack was a bit of an entrepreneur and was always looking for ways of bringing in additional income for his family. What started out as selling used items at flea markets, turned into a small business. Jack soon obtained a business license to allow him to attend auctions to bid on and purchase merchandise at wholesale prices. Soon, Jack purchased a canopy that was installed on a track on the passenger side of the van. This was used to provide shade when they sold their merchandise at the flea markets.

Jack and Agnes always did everything together. They complimented each other in so many ways. They grew more and more in love as each year passed. No matter what the challenge, they overcame it by working together.

Agnes informed Jack of a firm located in New York that sold women's suits and pants suits. She discovered this information when she worked part-time selling women's clothes for a small distributor. With the money they managed to save from the flea market, they travelled to New York to purchase some merchandise. Jack investigated to find out where the show room was located. He and Agnes agreed not to drive to New York, but to take the bus. They left at six am and arrived in New York around nine thirty in the morning. The show room was located in one of the sky scrapers on Broadway. After looking at the available goods offered at the show room, Jack and Agnes wanted to know if the company had a larger selection. The manager told them a larger selection was available at the factory. The couple was given a business card and directions how to get to the factory. Agnes and Jack had to catch two subway trains to get to Far Rockaway and finally a place called Inwood. Agnes was in her domain. This place was like being in fashion heaven. She found many one of a kind garments. These items were discounted for additional savings.

After shopping, the articles were paid for and shipped via UPS to Jack and Agnes's home. They caught the subway trains back to New York city. They had dinner, attended an off broadway show and returned to Baltimore by bus later that evening.

Agnes had a display party at her home inviting co-workers from the Dept. of Education, and friends that worked at the Dept. of Social Services. Within two days, all of the merchandise was sold. Over two dozen ladies knit suits and pants suits were sold. Agnes held some suits for Jack's sisters and her sisters. The merchandise sold out immediately. Agnes also kept a suit for Jack's mother.

Jack found additional ways to make the van pay for itself. He took groups on trips for a reasonable rate. One of his best trips was a weekend in Up state New York by a jazz organization. He took a group of ten peolpe to a jazz festival. Each person paid sixty five dollars to Jack for the trip. In addition, the organization paid for Jack's motel room and his meals. The tickets for the shows were also included.

What started out as a big loss turned into an unexpected gain. The van was paying for itself. Jack continued to go to auctions and buying trips to secure merchandise to sell at the flea markets. Agnes concentrated mostly on the buying trips that involved ladies fashions and other clothing articles. This business venture turned out to be more than a part-time job. It provided them with additional income as well as a form of socialization.

Agnes enjoyed shopping for her friends and relatives and having the parties showing off her talents. She made many friends shopping for people. They trusted her judgement to find something fashionable and suitable. She left the bookkeeping to Jack because he was very good at it. Jack also developed a plan to market their new merchandise. When Agnes's friends took orders for a certain number of sales, they were able to get a free gift that usually resulted in an outfit for themselves. They were also very sucessful in moving the goods quickly because they extended credit to their customers. This consisted of half being paid at the time of the sale and the balance to be paid over a few pay periods. The down payment generally consisted of the cost of the merchandise. This worked out very well for the couple and for the customers. The customers also realized a savings on the merchandise because the store prices were much higher.

As time went on, Jack worked most of the flea market dates by himself. Agnes did not have the stamina to continue with her job at the school, her work at home and the buying trips. Jack did not mind this arrangement because he was always concerned about Agnes's health and her not exhausting herself. The flea market was an outlet for Jack. He enjoyed doing this very much. He met a lot of very interesting people at the flea market, and even if he did not have a profitable day he enjoyed being out meeting the people.

When Jack did not have the van out earning extra income, he was using it to take his family and friends on outings. One such trip was a visit to relatives in Philadelphia, Pa. Jack, Agnes, three of his sisters and their husbands attended a cousin's wedding anniversary. By using the van, family members did not have to drive three or more cars to the event. This was safer and it was also a way of bringing family members closer together.

CHAPTER SIXTEEN

...Balancing demands of Family, Job and Interests

Both, Jack and Agnes had a full plate when it came to the demands on their time. With three teenagers, it was not easy giving them the individual attention necessary for their growth and development and maintaining a full time job as well as other interests. Jack and Agnes shared responsibilities and supported each other to accomplish this task.

In addition to raising a family, Agnes was very involved in the activities at the school where she worked. Besides her normal duties, she was an advocate and mentor for her students and their parents. She was also there for her co-workers. Agnes was drained by the time she got home. Jack would let her sleep and get the rest she needed. He routinely prepared the meals and did much of the shopping. The two oldest girls helped out a lot with other chores around the house.

Agnes was also a confidant and advised many of her family members on problems and issues they dealt with. Although she was the youngest of her sibblings, she was there for them. She often provided moral support and gave advice on many subjects. She was a very mature and knowledgeable person for her age.

Jack knew she was very important to his immediate family, but was not always aware of the help she gave to others. She was the type of person that people felt comfortable sharing their most intimate secrets with. She was always there for family, extended family and many of her friends.

There was one co-worker (Jane) that she was a dear friend to. Jane was in a very abusive relationship and often needed someone to talk to. She often called Agnes after having a fight with her husband. Agnes was always available to talk things over with Jane and be a good listener. She did not make decisions that Jane needed to make for herself, but was there to help her. Eventually, Jane got out of the abusive relationship and credited Agnes for being there when she needed her. Agnes never turned her back on anyone that needed her help.

Jack was amazed to find out all the good things that his wife did for others, but not surprised. He always knew she was very special and grew more in love with her as time went on. Jack accepted the fact that he just had to share this angel with others. She often shopped for clothes for students at her school as if they were her own children. Jack realized that he was blessed to have such a giving person in his life.

The one thing Jack was constantly concerned about was Agnes's health. He noticed that she always seemed tired. Agnes was not overly concerned and thought she just needed to get more rest. Jack certainly did what he could to take some of the pressure off of Agnes. Jack would do most of the cooking and helped out with the housekeeping. He also enlisted the help of his children. They all had chores that they were responsible for; however, the girls felt that Jack Jr. was not pulling his load. His responsibilities were limited to taking out the trash and keeping the lawn cut. Keeping his room in order was also one of his duties but someone else would always have to check behind him.

One thing Agnes always had time for were her children. She was constantly a part of their lives. She cherished her family very much and was there for them, no matter what. There were not very many situations that she could not handle.

In addition to being there for her children, she helped anyone else that was in need of her special talents. She helped Jack's niece with her wedding plans. She made her wedding gown along with dresses for the bride's maids. Agnes was always taking on some sewing project for friends and relatives. When she was in the sewing mode, Jack took up the slack as far as meal preparation and other chores around the house. Sometimes, he would watch her while she worked on her sewing projects. She was very creative and talented in this area.

Coming of Age

Two of the children were now in high school and the youngest would be entering high school after the school year ended. Jack and Agnes talked to their oldest daughter about her plans for the future. Jack talked to Veronica(the oldest girl) about her plans for college. She did not seem all that interested in going to college at the time. Jack tried not to put too much pressure on her, but knew the importance of her continuing her education. He encouraged her to keep her grades up and stay focused on school. He explained to her that having a good education would certainly make any goals she had more attainable.

Agnes continued to juggle her schedule trying to keep up with all the demands placed on her. She got tired more frequently, and this gave Jack reason to be concerned. She just brushed it off, and told Jack not to worry. She promised to get more rest and take better care of herself. Agnes joked with Jack and told him he was like a mother hen(so protective). Jack smiled and held her in his arms.

Agnes did as she promised. She cut back on many of her activities. Agnes limited the number of sewing projects but continued to be very active at her school. It was so difficult for her to say no to anyone. Jack continued to support her by accepting more responsiblity of the home.

Veronica drops a bombshell

As Veronica's graduation date drew near, she decided not to attend college right away. She told her parents she was thinking about joining the Navy. Jack was furious, but had to handle this delicate situation very carefully. He informed his daughter that it was very difficult for a young black female in the service, especially the navy. Veronica explained to him that a navy recruiter shared with her how she could continue her education while serving her country. Jack knew that it would not be that easy. He explained to his daughter that there was no guarantee that she would get into the schools the navy promised. Veronica had a stubborn streak she inherited from both parents. After seeing that he was not able to change her mind, Jack decided to compromise with his daughter. He asked her to attend a local college for a year and if after a year she still wanted to join the navy she would have his blessing. Veronica agreed to this and decided to register at a local college.

CHAPTER SEVENTEEN

...Changes that leaves a family Devastated

After a year of college, Veronica talked to her parents about the decision she reached. She approached her father cautiously. Her grades for her first year of college were acceptable. She told him the decision she made concerning college. Jack listened without interrupting her. Veronica informed her father that she would like to join the navy. When Jack did speak, He simply said okay. You kept your end of the bargain by attending college for one year. Now, I will keep mine. You have my blessing. Veronica could not believe her ears. She was expecting a fight from her father.

Veronica Joins the Navy

The next couple of months were very difficult for the entire family. Jack and Agnes were very subdued now that their first born joined the navy. Jack Jr. and Marie missed their big sister very much.

They did not have her to tease or tell them what to do or not to do. Jack and Agnes prayed for her every night and asked God to protect her.

After three weeks of basic training, the letters came. For the first time in her life, Veronica did not have her parents to protect her. She was being yelled at, told what to do and when to do it by complete strangers. She also felt that she was being singled out and mistreated.

She thought she was prepared to handle the situation in the service because her dad used to yell a lot around the house. The difference was he loved and protected her.

Jack answered every letter and tried to give her the courage and confidence necessary to reach her objectives. Veronica now saw what the real world was like. This weighed heavily on Jack and Agnes. The concern was more visible with Agnes. At times, she seemed very distant. Jack noticed that Agnes was sleeping a lot and did not have much energy. He talked to her about taking vitamins to give her more energy. Agnes knew she was anemic and needed vitamins with iron.

Jack thought that Agnes was depressed and did everything he could to make her comfortable. Every evening when she came from work, she went straight to bed. Jack cooked dinner and asked the children to wake her to come eat. When Agnes came down to eat, she always thanked Jack for being so understanding. Jack noticed that Agnes was sleeping more than usual.

Finally, Jack and Agnes received some good news from Veronica. She would be completing basic training in Orlando, Florida. She hoped her parents would be able to attend the graduation exercises. Jack and Agnes had not taken a vacation for two years. Jack thought this would be an excellent opportunity to see his daughter and spend time with Agnes exploring Florida. He discussed his plans with Agnes and booked a flight and made hotel reservations for a week. This seemed to perk Agnes up. They talked about visiting Disney World and other sites in Orlando.

The happy couple were making arrangements for their trip. They asked Sandy(Agnes's sister) to stay at their home to watch the children. Jack paid for the airplane tickets and purchased items they needed for their trip. Both, Jack and Agnes were very excited about the trip. Jack requested vacation leave at the health department and Agnes did likewise on her job.

An Illness that changed their lives forever

Two weeks before departure, Agnes was once again feeling very tired and weak. She continued to go to work, and tried to hide her true feelings from Jack. She did not want anything to interfere with the trip they planned. She tried to mask her feelings by taking over the counter medication and getting plenty of rest.

Jack received a call on his job from the school secretary where Agnes worked. He was informed that his wife was ill and needed to go home. Jack immediately left work and went to Agnes's school. He picked her up and took her home. This was on a friday afternoon.

Jack told Agnes she needed to see a doctor. He called her doctor and made an appointment for Monday. Jack fixed her a meal and tucked her into bed. He stayed with her until the children arrived at home. He prepared their food and told them their mother was not feeling well. Jack continued to watch over Agnes for the rest of the evening.

The next morning Jack got up early to fix everyone's breakfast. He went back upstairs to wake Agnes up for her breakfast. Jack sat on the side of the bed and gently shook Agnes. She was slow to rise. As she sat up in the bed, Jack got the shock of his life. He tried not to alarm Agnes by what he saw. Her face was swollen and distorted. Jack calmly told her of her condition. He told her to get dressed because he was taking her to the hospital emergency room.

When Agnes was seen at the hospital the doctors immediately began to run tests on her. They finally called in a thoracic surgeon who ran tests and took extensive xrays. The doctor explained to Jack and Agnes that she would need to be hospitalized on Monday to run further tests. The surgeon shared the xray results with Jack and Agnes and told them it revealed a large mass in the chest cavity. He was not prepared to say anything more until the tests were run.

Jack admitted Agnes in the hospital on the following Monday. The doctors began to run tests and rule out certain conditions. After a couple of days of tests, Agnes called Jack to the hospital. Jack went to the hospital with Marie and Jack Jr. When they arrived on Agnes's floor, She asked Jack to hold her hand and they all walked down the hospital hallway. Agnes told her family that she had bad news. She looked at Jack and said, "I have cancer" Jack, Agnes and two of their children wept openly. Jack was truly devastated by the news. Nothing could have prepared him for such a shock. After weeping for awhile, Agnes gathered her family together and began to pray. She said we have to face this illness and try to overcome it. Jack tried very hard to digest the news he received. What he knew about cancer at that time was comparable to being given a death sentence.

Decision Time

Jack and Agnes met with the doctor to see what their options were. After discussing the possibilities, it was recommended that surgery be performed. The surgeon discussed the risks that were involved. Agnes wanted to have the surgery. A date was set for the surgery. Jack took Agnes home to wait for the scheduled date of surgery. After talking things over with her immediate family, Agnes contacted her siblings and told them of her illness. Everyone was devastated to hear such dreadful news.

Jack was more attentive and supportive than he had ever been if that was possible. He could not understand how something like this could happen to Agnes. She never smoked or abused her body in any way. She did not drink alcholol nor did she do anything that could be considered detrimental to her well being. If Jack could trade places with her he certainly would. He felt strongly at the time that God had really turned his back on his family. How could he let this happen to an angel like Agnes.

Surgery Performed

Agnes was admitted to the hospital the evening before her surgery. Her surgery was scheduled for seven thirty in the morning. The surgery took hours. Jack waited what seemed like a life time for some news from the doctor. Finally, around noon time the surgeon came in the waiting room to see Jack. Jack was very anxious and prayed that the surgery was successful. The surgeon told Jack that the cancer was wrapped around vital organs and arteries. It was virtually impossible to remove it without causing damage. She could have bled to death on the table if we had removed it said the surgeon. The doctor informed Jack that the team was unable to remove any of the cancer. Jack could not believe what he was hearing. He tried to process the information he was given. Jack felt his whole world was crashing in on him. He felt Agnes went through major surgery with nothing to show but an ugly scar.

After sitting in the waiting room trying to compose himself, Jack went to comfort his wife. Agnes was still groggy from the anesthetics. Jack gently held her. When she finally spoke, she asked Jack if he talked with her doctor. Jack responded that he had. Agnes seemed so calm as she told Jack what the next step would be. The surgeon referred her to an oncologist for treatment. She showed such strength and courage that Jack could not do any less. He knew her faith was strong, but was amazed that she could handle this situation so well. She was not bitter at all. Jack tried to hide his true feelings from Agnes. He was upset, angry and obviously very hurt but did not want to show this in front of his ailing wife. Agnes could handle most situations, but could not stand to see Jack in any pain. Agnes would be in the hospital for awhile recuperating from the surgery.

Meanwhile Jack divided his time between home, work and the hospital. He visited Agnes everyday she was hospitalized and stayed there until visiting hours were over. Agnes met the oncologist that would be treating her. She set up a time for Jack to meet with the doctor. Jack met the doctor that would be treating her cancer. He explained the risks that were involved and possible reactions and side effects of the medication. This doctor was very pleasant and informative but realistic. He assured Jack and Agnes that he would be treating the cancer very agressively but cautioned against any unrealistic results or instant recovery.

Agnes Starts Her Cancer Treatment

Initially, Agnes cancer treatment started with chemotheraphy. The doctor placed her on a combination of drugs that were given intravenously. Agnes was hospitalized when she got this treatment. Agnes was always very weak after the chemo. When Jack picked her up from the hospital, he took her home and cared for her like a baby.

He did everything he could to take her mind off her sickness. After she regained her strength, the doctor had her to come in to be evaluated. After the first few treatments, there was little or no change in the tumor. The doctor changed the combination of drugs to see what effect it would have on the cancer.

After treating the cancer for a while, he came up with a combination of drugs that the tumor responded to. When Jack took Agnes for her evaluation after treatments with the new drug regimen, the chest xray revealed that the tumor was indeed smaller. This was the best news Jack and Agnes had for sometime. This change did not come without a cost. All of Agnes's hair came out and the chemo treatments left her very weak.

It was difficult for her to eat and keep food on her stomach. Jack was very creative in getting her to eat. He prepared fruit juices mixed with brewer's yeast and wheat germ. This concoction helped her to keep food on her stomach as well as increasing her appitite. Agnes watched Jack as he prepared food for her and the family. She told Jack how blessed she was to have him to care for her. Jack countered by saying he was the one who was blessed to have an angel in his life. When Agnes felt better, Jack asked her to put on big ear rings and make up. He held her and told her he always wanted a ball headed woman. Agnes laughed until tears ran down her face. Her smile was as bright as the morning sun. This helped both of them to cope with a situation that was anything but a laughing matter.

Cancer is in Remission

After months of treatment, Agnes and Jack learned from her doctor that the tumor had shrunk considerably. Agnes regained some of her strength. Her doctor decided to refer her for a series of radiation treatments. The cancer continued to shrink to the size of a fifty cents piece. Agnes and Jack did not take anything for granted. They were cautiously optimistic. Agnes was now on disability and devoted most of her time to getting well and fighting this illness. The doctors were very pleased to see the results, but knew Agnes was not out of the woods. They treated many cancer patients with similar results only to have the cancer return a short time later.

Six months later, there still was no sign of the cancer. Agnes was feeling very well considering the ordeal she was going through. Her hair grew back lovlier than ever. Jack and Agnes talked constantly about life and sharing so many wonderful moments together. They cherished every moment they had together. Agnes spent time talking with her children and letting them know how much she loved them and how much they meant to her. Jack and Agnes spent hours talking to each other in bed before they fell asleep.

Agnes always prayed and never doubted God and his ability to put things in order. She was very religious and maintained her faith through it all. She grew even closer to the people she loved. The bond she had with her siblings, her aunts, uncles and cousins was strengthened. Agnes was like a magnet that drew people close to her.

Her many friends and well wishers were sending her cards and lovely notes. She had the chance to see her oldest daughter in her Navy uniform. Agnes was really counting her blessings.

The Cancer Returns

It was once again time for Agnes to return for her check up. The night before she was scheduled to see the doctor she told Jack she would like to talk to him. Agnes and Jack were lying in bed and she told him she was very frightened. Jack asked her why she was so frightened. Agnes informed Jack that the cancer had returned. "How do you know that"? Jack replied. You don't get your xrays until tomorrow. Agnes said, "Jack I can feel the cancer". With that a chill came over Jack. He caressed her and they prayed. Jack held Agnes until they both fell asleep.

After the chest xrays, Agnes's greatest fears were realized. The cancer had indeed returned. The doctor informed her that she would have to undergo more chemotheraphy. The cancer had returned with a vengeance. The drug regimen that was used to halt the cancer before would prove to be ineffective this time. Agnes underwent more combinations of drugs and radiation. The chemicals and radiation treatment took its toll on Agnes. She was growing weaker and weaker. Her body could not take any more treatment for awhile. Her doctor stopped the treatment so she could regain some strength.

Even in her declining health, Agnes was the same caring, giving and considerate individual. She handled her sickness with such dignity and her faith was undying. Seeing her strength, determination and positive attitude had a very sobering affect on Jack. He was there for her every step of the way. His love for her was unconditional. He loved her so much and felt so helpless.

Taking A Break

Jack wanted to take Agnes's mind off of her sickness. He felt they both could benefit from a short trip. He asked Agnes if you were to take a short trip, Where would you like to go? Agnes did not have to think twice before she answered the Bahamas. It was close enough to reach the destination in a few hours without her getting tired. They would be among friends that were as close as family members and she loved the peace and beauty of Paradise Island.

Jack booked their flights and made the hotel reservations. He planned the trip for five days, because he did not want it to be too hard on Agnes. The trip was scheduled in April,1984. Jack called" Sistah" in the Bahamas to inform her that he and Agnes would be coming soon." Sistah" told Jack that she would pick them up at the airport.

Jack and Agnes left on an early morning flight that arrived in the Bahamas before noon. They were met there by their friend(Sistah). She exchanged greetings with the couple and drove them to their hotel. She informed them that she would contact them later. Jack understood that she had a business to run and told her that he would be looking forward to her call.

Jack and Agnes decided to have lunch while they waited for check- in time at the hotel. Jack asked Agnes how she felt? He was surprised at the answer he received. Agnes felt better than she had for some time. She attributed it to the fresh air and the warm sun. She was able to breathe much easier. Agnes was suddenly relieved of all stress. Jack asked her if she felt like taking a stroll. "Yes, she replied." They went for a short walk and returned to check in at the hotel.

When they settled in their room, they decided to take a nap. A few hours later, Jack received another surprise. When he woke up, Agnes was up and had her shower. She was invigorated and seemed like a new person. Jack told her it was good to see her with so much energy. She said, "It must be the air". I haven't had any problems breathing. The stress was also gone. What would you like to do Jack?

The couple decided to go out and pick up a home cooked meal and return to the hotel. "Sistah" shared with them on previous visits where they could get home cooked meals at very reasonable prices. Agnes informed Jack that she did not want to take the ride on the ferry from Paradise Island to Nassau, but would rather take a cab. She looked at him and laughed. I'm not feeling that good that I want to chance riding on those shakey boats. Jack smiled and replied, "As you wish my lady."

After crossing the bridge, the first stop for them was Bay Street. They got out of the taxi and stopped by the straw market. Jack purchased a hat and Agnes picked up a shirt dress from their friend(Sistah). She owned a thriving business in the straw market. Jack asked if the take out restaurant was still in the same place. But of course, Sistah stated. Jack and Agnes walked the short distance to Frank's Place. You could smell the food before you reached his establishment. He served some of the best food on the Island. One could choose from American or Caribbean menus. Jack ordered something from both menus.

They returned to the hotel and had a delectable meal at one fifth the cost of hotel food. After their meal, Jack and Agnes sat out on their balcony and listened to music. After spending a couple of hours watching the stars and enjoying the beautiful sounds, they retired for the evening.

The next morning Jack and Agnes got up very early. They had a light breakfast at poolside on the hotel grounds. After breakfast, they caught a taxi to the other side of the bridge. Under the bridge were fruit vendors and other merchandise stands. The couple purchased fruits to take back to the hotel with them. When they returned, Agnes made a delicious fruit salad. They changed to their bathing suits and spent the rest of the morning on the beach. Agnes was as happy as a child on Christmas morning. She walked on the beach spinning around like a top. Jack had not seen her this happy for some time. Later that evening Jack took Agnes to see one of the Native Shows at a popular night spot on the Island. Afterwards, they spent a few hours in the casino on Paradise Island.

On the third day, the couple decided to shop for family and friends. They bought gifts at the straw market and duty free shops all over the Island. They shopped for most of the day. While they were out, they had a big lunch at a very popular Bahamian Restaurant called the Bahamian Kitchen. Their food was as tasty as Frank's Place but slightly more expensive. Jack made one last stop at one of the rum shops before returning to the hotel. When they arrived at the hotel, they changed into something comfortable and had a night cap. Jack had rum and coke and Agnes had a ginger ale. Jack looked at Agnes and told her they were really blessed to have each other. They toasted and held each other for hours like they did when they first met. The couple rested for a while, then enjoyed the calypso entertainment provided by the hotel on the ground level.

On the fourth and last full day the couple would spend on the Island, they began their day at seven thirty in the morning. It started with a light breakfast at the hotel. Afterwards, Jack and Agnes travelled from Paradise Island to downtown Nassau. They shopped for last minute gifts and souvenirs. They stopped by the straw market and picked up a couple of souvenir Tee shirts from their friend(Sistah). "Sistah" informed them that she would pick them up around six in the evening to have dinner and spend some time at her house. When Jack and his sisters travelled to Nassau they were always invited to her house for dinner.

Jack and Agnes had lunch at the Bahamian Kitchen before returning to their hotel. After arriving at the hotel, the couple decided to just chill out on the beach. Jack positioned the lounge chairs close to the entertainment. There were steel bands and Soca music on the beach. This turned out to be one of the most enjoyable afternoons the couple had in years. Agnes did not show any signs of her illness. For this period of time, her breathing was much better and she was not getting as tired. Jack and Agnes returned to their room to wait for" Sistah's" arrival.

Spending an Evening with a Friend

Agnes and Jack were dressed and listening to music when a knock came at the door. They were greeted by the smiling face of their dear friend. When they arrived at her house," Sistah's" family were putting on the finishing touches of the big dinner. Agnes and Jack exchanged greetings with "Sistah's" two lovely teenage daughters. They were also greeted by two of "Sistah's" sisters. Everything was so lovely and elegant. Everyone chatted and caught up on the news since their last visit.

"Sistah" informed Jack and Agnes that dinner was ready to be served. She smiled and said, "I hope you came with a big appetite". She prepared a feast. Jack and Agnes knew they were in for a treat.

The menu was a Bahamian delight. It consisted of Grouper fish, fried Red fish, peas and rice, Conch salad, Conch fritters, lobster salad and crabs. Macaroni and cheese, garden salad and stewed chicken. The dessert tray was very rich with black cake, fruit salad, coconut candy and pastries. Jack said a lovely grace and the feast began.

Jack had a good appetite as usual, but the surprise was to see Agnes really eating and enjoying the food. Her appetite was not as good since her illness, but since she had been in the Bahamas she was eating everything in sight. Everyone was very pleased to see her doing so well under the circumstances. This was indeed a happy time for all.

After dinner, the couple talked with "Sistah" and her family. "Sistah" drove them back to Paradise Island where they stopped at the casino." Sistah" watched as Jack and Agnes tried their luck. Jack was there about ten minutes before he hit a small jackpot for five hundred dollars. Jack decided not to press his luck, and left a winner. "Sistah" and Agnes sat on a wall outside the casino and talked some more. Jack thanked her for everything and told her to keep them in her prayers. They said their goodbyes and returned to the hotel. Jack and Agnes finished packing and spent their last night sitting on the balcony of their hotel room watching the cruise ships go by. The calypso and soca music was blasting as the ships passed. It was a wonderful time they had on this short but joyous vacation.

Returning Home

Jack and Agnes got up early the next morning and had a light breakfast. Their flight was at noon. After breakfast, Jack and Agnes went for a short walk around Paradise Island. The couple checked out of their hotel and caught a taxi to the airport. They picked up a few items at the duty free shops, paid their departure tax and waited for their flight.

Their flight was on time and left as scheduled. The take off was very smooth, and after the flight levelled off Jack took pictures of the Islands. Midway through the flight the plane ran into rough weather. The pilot decided to climb over the rough weather. Unfortunately, he had to start his descent in a thunder storm. At this point, the turbulence picked up and was really very rough. It felt like riding in a truck without any shocks. This went on for some time. Then, suddenly the plane dropped and the passengers became very alarmed. The pilot came over the PA system and announced that we were going through some rough turbulence. Right after that announcement, the plane ride really got rough. Agnes looked at Jack and said," I thought I was going to die from cancer not get killed in a plane crash". Jack did not respond right away, then they both started to laugh. Shortly, after that the plane levelled off and the pilot continued his descent. When the plane finally touched down, everyone on board clapped and yelled a sigh of relief.

When Jack and Agnes reached their home, they were met at the door by two of their children, their niece and Agnes' sister(Sandy). Everyone was so happy to see Jack and Agnes. "How was the trip mommy" asked Marie. Sandy told Agnes she looked like a picture of health. Jack Jr. asked his parents what gifts did they bring back? Jack and Agnes responded by taking the gifts out of the bags and giving them out. Sandy started to cry and told Agnes she had not seen her look this well in a long time. Jack and Agnes were touched by all the love and affection being shown. They embraced as their children giggled and Sandy said look at the love birds.

Jack and Agnes shared their vacation experience with their families and friends. Everyone was so pleased to hear that the couple had such a wonderful time In their private moments, Jack and Agnes faced the reality of the uphill battle that lies ahead. With the return of the cancer, they both knew that they would need all of the faith, strength and courage they could muster.

CHAPTER EIGHTEEN

Agnes Faces The Fight Of Her Life

A couple of weeks after the vacation, Agnes returned to the oncologist for evaluation. The examination revealed that the cancer was active once again. This meant more treatments of chemotherapy and possibly radiation. Agnes knew what she faced. She dreaded the thought of having to go through this experience again. Not so much for herself, but she was concerned about the affect it would have on Jack and the rest of her family. Agnes had such a strong faith that prepared her to face whatever was necessary to conquer this sickness. It was just like Agnes to be more concerned about the impact this would have on Jack and her children. Next to her love of God, her family was the most important thing in her life.

Agnes wanted to get well more than anything else so she could be there to enjoy and protect her family. She also accepted the fact that if it was God's will that she lose her battle with cancer, she was prepared to do so. Agnes had made her peace with God. She also knew that Jack was a very spiritual person. What she did not know was that Jack prayed to God to give him the strength to endure and cope with this illness.

The doctor tried many combinations of chemicals, but this time they seemed to have little or no effect on the cancer. It was now five months after the vacation and the drugs were taking its toll on Agnes' health. The treatment left her in a weakened condition. Agnes did not have the strength to travel to St Pius parish;therefore, Jack took her to a church that was closer to their home. In spite of the ordeal Agnes was going through, the couple remained optimistic about her outcome. Neither Jack nor Agnes contemplated the idea of her not being able to survive her bout with this terrible disease.

The cancer was growing stronger and faster, and the chemo left Agnes very weak. Because of her weakened condition Agnes was not a good candidate for more radiation treatments. For the first time, Agnes had doubts about being able to survive her illness. Still, she managed to put on a very pleasant face for Jack and the rest of her family. Jack felt her pain and admired her for the strength and courage she showed.

Once again, her doctor suspended her treatments until she regained some strength. Two or three weeks later Agnes had an appointment to see her doctor. Jack and Agnes spoke to her doctor about the bruising she had on her arms. Because of her small veins, it was difficult for the hospital staff to obtain blood or give her the intravenous medication. Agnes was fitted with a device to alleviate this problem.

Agnes Condition Worsens

The cancer was now growing at an alarming rate. Her doctor decided to try other experimental drugs to see if this would impede the growth of the tumor. Agnes was now being admitted to the hospital for longer than the usual one day stay. Jack continued with his usual routine, caring for his children, going to work on a daily basis and stopping by the hospital every day Agnes was there.

On her next hospital visit, the doctors decided to insert a Hickman Catheter into her chest. Jack was trained by the nursing staff how to clean this device. It had to be flushed daily with a saline solution. Jack had to use a large syringe to do this every morning. Jack would get up at five thirty every morning and prepare everyone's breakfast. He then took care of Agnes's nursing needs and prepared for work. He never missed a day of work during this period of Agnes's illness.

Agnes was growing weaker and weaker. When she did not feel well enough to go to church, she would call her priest and talk to him. One Sunday morning after the morning mass there was a knock at the door. Jack was in the process of preparing breakfast for Agnes. With his apron still on, he opened the door. He was very surprised to see Father Conley. The priest asked Jack how things were going? He came to see Agnes, but had an opportunity to see the attention and care Jack was providing for his wife. Agnes was sitting up in bed as Jack showed the priest to her room. He talked and prayed with Agnes while Jack completed the breakfast. When Father Conley came back downstairs, he wanted to talk to Jack. He asked Jack how he was coping with the situation? He was amazed that Jack was providing the nursing care as well as assisting with the activities of daily living. The priest asked Jack if this was too much of a burden on him. Jack paused for a moment and replied, "When one has been as good as Agnes has I don't see her as a burden at all". I do this because I love her with all of my heart and I'll do whatever is necessary to care for her and make her comfortable. I can't do any less. I just pray to God to give me the strength to continue. The priest told Jack that he was an amazing individual and was truly blessed.

It is now November, of 1984 and Agnes was in and out of the hospital. She was in constant pain but you would never know it. When visited by family and friends, she always managed to make everyone else feel better. As sick as she was, she always managed to show her pleasant attitude and winning personality. The only time she would show any indication of how sick she really was happened to be when she and Jack were alone. Because she showed so much courage, Jack never let her or his children see him when he was really hurting. It was tougher during the night. Agnes was unable to breathe when she laid flat. Jack propped her up with pillows to make her as comfortable as he could. Afterwards, he went downstairs to the kitchen pretending to get a snack. Jack found his way to the basement and cried his eyes out. He wanted so much to be able to help Agnes, but felt powerless to do anything about her condition.

Jack contacted her doctor to inform him of her difficulty breathing. Agnes was placed on oxygen. She had oxygen in the home as well as a portable container when she had to travel. On her next hospital visit Agnes was given more bad news. Jack and Agnes was informed that the cancer had metastasized. The doctor talked to Jack and Agnes about her condition and decided to stop the treatment because it was not helping at this time. Agnes was not strong enough to withstand the effects of the chemo.

Agnes Succumbs

December,1984 Agnes was resting at home. Jack was very attentive and was doing all he could to make his wife comfortable. He only left the house to shop, pick up the children from their part-time jobs and go to work. Jack and Agnes' families knew he needed some respite and offered to help. Jack never admitted that he needed any help. He only knew that his wife needed him and he was there. Agnes's sister(Sandy) would come over while Jack was at work, but Agnes would not let her do but so much. Jack's mother prepared home made chicken soup and brought it over to Agnes. Agnes felt very secure when Jack was by her side. She was not afraid when he was near her.

Jack was at work one day and Agnes needed to be picked up from an appointment. One of Agnes's cousins was very glad to assist. Jack arrived at home and started preparing for the evening meal.

Agnes was not feeling very well and went to bed. Jack took her meal to the bedroom. Agnes looked at Jack and told him she was really blessed to have him to care for her like he did. Jack responded by saying," It's not every day that one gets to care for an angel".

Later on that night, Agnes could not sleep. She was very uncomfortable when she tried to lie flat. It was extremely difficult for her to breathe. Jack propped her up and made sure that her oxygen was on. The next day Agnes was admitted to the hospital. When Jack stopped by the hospital on his way from work, He noticed that Agnes was resting comfortably in the hospital bed. In the adjustable bed, Agnes was more comfortable. Jack told Agnes he would take down their large bed and order a hospital bed before she was discharged. Jack stayed with her until visiting hours were over. The following morning, Jack called a hospital supply and equipment company and ordered the bed. This was on a Friday Dec.21. The bed would be delivered on Monday Dec.24.

Jack went by the hospital on his lunch hour Friday afternoon and informed Agnes that he ordered the hospital bed. She smiled and asked Jack to hold her. Jack held her for awhile and told her he would stop by after work. On Saturday, Jack took the children to visit their mother. She was also visited by her sisters and aunts. Jack drove his children to work and came back later Saturday evening to spend the rest of the day with Agnes. She had to go for a number of tests. She was exhausted when she was brought back to the room. Jack put his arms around her until she fell asleep. Agnes woke up for a short time and Jack told her he would come by early Sunday to be with her. He let her rest and went home to get some sleep.

Jack arrived at the hospital early Sunday morning and Agnes was not in her room. He was told by one of the nurses that she was undergoing more tests. After forty five minutes, Agnes was returned to her room. She told Jack she was not feeling very well. Then, another nurse came into the room and told Agnes she needed to take some blood to get her oxygen blood gas. Jack stayed with Agnes the rest of the day. Agnes was sitting in a chair and Jack held his wife. She told Jack she was tired and cold. Jack held her and noticed that her arms were very cold and clammy. Jack told the nurse that Agnes was not feeling well. The nurse and the nurse's assistant helped her to get back in bed. Jack did not have a good feeling, but he passed it off as Agnes just being tired.

About four thirty that afternoon, the nurse called Agnes's doctor and gave him her test results. The doctor asked to speak to Jack. Jack picked up the phone at the nurse's station to talk to the doctor. The doctor informed Jack that Agnes was a very sick young lady. He also said that she had been a model patient. He was trying to prepare Jack for the inevitable. Jack was informed that Agnes would not survive her bout with cancer. Jack was very quiet on the phone for a moment and wanted to know approximately when Agnes would succumb. The doctor told Jack he was not expecting her to survive through the evening. Jack did not expect to hear that. He was prepared to hear that she would die around late January or February. Jack almost dropped the phone. He then thanked the doctor for caring for Agnes.

Jack went back into the room to be with Agnes as she was drifting into sleep. Jack knew he had to go to pick up the children. He made a few telephone calls to Agnes older sister and called his mother. When Agnes's sister arrived at the hospital, he asked her to stay with her while he picked up the children. Jack went to the department store where Marie and Jack Jr. worked and picked them up. He informed them that their mother was very sick and not expected to survive. When they arrived at the hospital, they were crying before they could get to the room.

Jack went over to the bed where a number of relatives had gathered. They all held hands and began to pray. Some of the relatives would leave to make room for other relatives that were in the waiting room. After everyone had a chance to visit their loved one, Jack and one of Agnes 's older sisters were the only two people left in the room. They stood by her bed trying to comfort her as she slipped in and out of a coma. Jack rubbed her face and held her hand. His wife, friend and soul mate was dying. He heard her heavy breathing and saw her body slowly stretching out. As the life was leaving her body, He heard her utter her last two words which were "Jesus, Jesus" and with that she took her last breath. It was eight fifteen Sunday evening. December 23, 1984

Christmas without an Angel

The next few days Jack spent making funeral arrangements for his wife. He woke up early Christmas morning not realizing it was Christmas. He had been so consumed by Agnes's sickness that he did not put up Christmas decorations. Jack played one of his and Agnes's favorite Christmas albums by Mahalia Jackson. He listened to the tunes that gave him so much pleasure and had a very soothing and therapeutic effect on him. When the song "What Can I Give" came up Jack broke down. He realized that this was the first Christmas in two decades that he would spend without his angel.

Jack quickly gathered his composure so he would not wake up his children who were sleeping upstairs. His oldest daughter had arrived home on leave from the military. She was a big help to Jack and her brother and sister. Jack knew he had to be strong not only for his immediate family but also for Agnes's family. She was very special and the youngest of all her sibblings.

Jack had appointments with the funeral director and the priest at Agnes's church. After the meeting with the funeral director, Jack met Hazel(Agnes's older sister) at ST. Pius V Catholic Church. Jack talked with Father Conley for quite a while. He had become very fond of Jack and Agnes and the love and devotion they had for each other. He made mention of how Jack would bring Agnes to church when she was strong enough to attend. He could not get the picture out of his mind when Jack opened his door with his apron still on that Sunday morning.

During the conversation with Jack, the priest was reviewing the church records. He discovered something that he thought was unusual. He shared with Jack that Agnes went through all of her sacrements at St. Pius V. They were baptism, confirmation, matrimony and now burial rites. He thought this was indeed special. Jack had grown very fond of this priest and not being Catholic he had a good understanding of the Catholic faith. Jack felt much better after his meeting with father Conley.

The Funeral

Before any public viewing, the funeral director sent a car to pick up Jack to make sure everything was satisfactory. Jack was very nervous about keeping this appointment. He was going to view the body of the closest individual in his life. This was much different than viewing an older relative like his grandmother or grandfather. This was his wife, the mother of his children, a person whom he shared his most intimate secrets with. She was still a relatively young woman who had so much more to give.

When Jack arrived at the funeral home, his heart started to beat very rapidly. As he approached Agnes's coffin the nervousness subsided. He looked at her face and was relieved. She looked so peaceful. She was simply beautiful. He knew she was not in any pain and no longer suffering. Jack thought about the pain she endured for the last two years and could now see only peace and tranquility.

The day of the funeral was the longest day of Jack's life. Generally, the funerals at this church were in the morning. Because of the holiday and other services scheduled at the church the funeral was held at night. When Jack and his children arrived at the church, people were standing all around the building. The church was filled to capacity. Friends, co-workers, and interested on lookers were standing in all the isles. The church was decorated with all of the Christmas arrangements. Jack thought, how fitting for saying farewell to an angel.

Father Conley presided over the service. Two of Jacks's brothers participated in the service at the invitation from father Conley. Jack's oldest and youngest brothers were both Baptist ministers. Jack's oldest daughter(Veronica) read bible verses. This was one very moving funeral service. When a friend sang "Ave Maria" You could hear the sobs throughout the church. Jack tried to comfort his children as they all wept openly. When father Conley eulogized Agnes, he spoke of all the lives that were touched by such an incredible and loving person. After everyone spoke, the mood changed from sorrow to joy. It was so appropriate that this service happened during the Christmas season because of the gift of joy and love Agnes gave to all that she came into contact with. It was indeed celebrating the life of an angel.

Picking up The Pieces

The funeral of his beloved is now over and Jack is faced with the difficult task of putting his life back together. The impact of Agnes's disease and ultimately her death left Jack feeling empty and numb. His daughters were coping with the loss of their mother much better than their brother. Jack was very concerned about his sixteen year old son, who took the death of his mother very hard. He was always a charming and happy go lucky child, but the death of his mother left him very bitter. It also weakened his faith and belief in God. Jack Jr. told his father he could not understand how God could take such a good person like his mother at such a young age by a horrible disease like cancer. Jack discussed the situation with father Conley who decided to help keep Jack Junior involved in church activities and counseling services.

As for Jack, he did what he did all during Agnes's illness: He went to work. Jack buried himself in his work. Shortly after the funeral, Jack went back to work at the Health Dept. When he returned, his co-workers informed him that they did not realize that his wife was that ill. His supervisor was amazed that Jack was at work almost daily under the kind of pressure and stress he was going through. Jack was a supervisor in his department and his work did not suffer at all. They could not understand how Jack was able to function under those conditions. What they did not know was Jack's prayers were answered by God. When Agnes first became ill, Jack prayed and asked God to give him the strength and the courage to deal with her illness. Jack understood that God took his burden and made it light. There was no way Jack could have gone through this period of his life the way he did without divine help and guidance.

Agnes: A Gift that keeps Giving

It is now February, 1985 two months after Agnes's death. Jack followed the same routine. He got up in the morning, went to work, came straight home to virtually an empty house. He prepared dinner, listened to the news and retreated to his bedroom. Then, he picked up a picture of his late wife and grieved. Marie and Junior were involved in after school activities or working their part time jobs. Jack had been crying himself to sleep everyday since Agnes's death. No one knew how much he really missed his wife. On outward appearances, he was friendly and very dignified. Inside, he was going through a private hell.

Jack had not accepted Agnes's death up to this time. He rushed home thinking that she would return and be there waiting for him. Then, it hit him that she was gone, all he had was his memories. Jack was hurting and no one could help him. He was not willing at this time to share his feelings with anyone. The only person that had any idea what he was going through was his daughter, Marie. She could hear him sobbing some nights. Jack would try to play it off like he had a cough or a cold.

It was a very cold night towards the end of February and Jack was sitting up in bed looking at Agnes's picture. Once again, he cried himself to sleep holding her picture. About two o'clock in the morning Jack could hear someone softly calling his name. He smelled a familiar perfume and felt someone gently shaking him. Jack sat up in bed and saw a glowing light at the end of his bed. He heard the voice call his name again. The image of Agnes slowly came into focus. Jack rubbed his eyes to make sure they were not playing tricks on him. He saw a radiant smile on Agnes's face. In her soft and pleasant voice she said, "Jack, We have to talk." You can not go on like this. I am okay, but you have to let go. I can not move on to my destination with you holding on to me like this. Soon, I will be with the Holy Father. We had a very good life together, but you must continue with your life. Jack replied, "Agnes, I need you so much, I miss you, please stay with me". I don't know if I can go on without you. I don't want to go on without you. "Jack, God still has a plan for you." Your work here is not done. You must continue to live for yourself and the children. I am so grateful that God allowed us to meet and share a life together. I am at peace. I know you are hurting now, but I pray that it will turn to joy when you focus on the wonderful memories of a life time we shared together. The time has come for you to move on with your life. At that moment, Jack felt peace come over him. Agnes said," Please take care of yourself and remember I will always love you." I must leave now. Agnes began to slowly disappear. The glowing light began to fade as Jack fell asleep again.

The next morning, Jack remembered the message that Agnes brought to him and a burden was lifted off his shoulders. He now accepted the fact that Agnes was gone and is alright. It is now time for Jack to get on with his life. Jack thought to himself, even in her death Agnes found a way to continue to give comfort to her loved one. Jack thought about the first time he saw Agnes and all the memories of their life together. He then put his thoughts in the form of a poem for his wife.

The Day I Saw An Angel

As a teen when you came into my world,
I could see an angel inside a little girl.
I knew on that balmy spring day,
My life would change in every way.
I watched you from a distance, then got the nerve to speak,
The smile that came upon your face was such a delightful treat.
As time grew on when we became as one,
I was the earth and you were my morning sun.
We were inseparable for a love that was meant to be,
A story of love and friendship that is older than the sea.
As our family grew, I certainly knew that the lord had blessed us so,
He had placed an angel in our mist, what a precious gift to bestow.

When life dealt us a curve or two,

Your calmness and faith would pull us through.

Then came your declining health which you faced with such strength and courage,

As you laid on your dying bed, a light began to glow above your head.

You drifted into a deep, deep sleep'

I could see your wings sprouting right through the sheets.

I knew at that moment without a doubt,

God was reclaiming his angel he had only loaned out.

ABOUT THE AUTHOR

The author was born in Baltimore, Maryland the seventh of ten children. He was educated in the Baltimore City Public School System and graduated from Morgan State University. He has provided thirty years of service to the Baltimore community in the area of health and human services. Six years with the Anti-Poverty Program and twenty four years with the Baltimore City Health Department.

This experience served him well. He was exposed to real life struggles of residents in the various communities and their ability to cope with a society in transition. He has written about a variety of topics using a sensitive and human approach. This is evidenced in his first published book of poems. "Poems Reflections The Black Experience" published by 1stBooks Library.